Twayne's English Authors Series

Sylvia E. Bowman, *Editor*

INDIANA UNIVERSITY

William Blake

TEAS 202

William Blake, *a drawing by John Linnell, about 1825*

WILLIAM BLAKE

By VICTOR N. PAANANEN
Michigan State University

TWAYNE PUBLISHERS

A DIVISION OF G. K. HALL & CO., BOSTON

Library of Congress Cataloging in Publication Data

Paananen, Victor N
   William Blake.

   (Twayne's English author series)
   Bibliography: p. 163–68.
   Includes index.
   1. Blake, William, 1757-1827.   2. Poets, English —
19th century — Biography.
   PR4146.P3   821'.7   76-45352
   ISBN 0-8057-6672-3

MANUFACTURED IN THE UNITED STATES OF AMERICA

To the Memory of my Father

<small>Niles Henry Paananen</small>
(1910–1956)

Contents

About the Author

Preface

Acknowledgments

Chronology

1. Life and Times   15

2. Poetry and Perception: The Two Tracts on Religion
   and *The Book of Urizen*   29

3. *Poetical Sketches*   48

4. *The Marriage of Heaven and Hell*   53

5. *The French Revolution* and *America*   61

6. *Visions of the Daughters of Albion*   70

7. *Songs of Innocence and of Experience*   74

8. *The Four Zoas*   88

9. Manuscript Poems   113

10. *Milton*   119

11. *Jerusalem*   133

Conclusion   152

Notes and References   157

Selected Bibliography   163

Index   169

About the Author

Victor N. Paananen is Associate Professor of English, and Associate Chairman, at Michigan State University. Dr. Paananen received the Bachelor of Arts *magna cum laude* from Harvard. After a period as fidelity and surety bond underwriter, he earned the Master of Arts and Doctor of Philosophy degrees from the University of Wisconsin where he held the University Fellowship. He has previously taught at Wofford College and at Williams College.

Dr. Paananen has specialized in the intellectual backgrounds of British Romanticism. He examined the relationship between traditional skepticism and the poetry of Lord Byron and Robert Browning in his doctoral dissertation, "Byron and Browning: The Aesthetics of Skepticism" (Wisconsin, 1967). Since then he has studied the contributions of Anglican Evangelicalism and other eighteenth-century religious movements (such as Sweden-borgianism and Unitarianism) to the thought and art of English Romanticism and has investigated British political thought of the nineteenth century. He has published articles on Lord Byron and the Anglican Evangelical Martin Madan and is the author of two articles, "Robert Burns" and "Leigh Hunt," for the *Biographical Dictionary of Modern British Radicals*.

Preface

This book, a brief, introductory account of the writings of William Blake, appears at a time when Blake studies are characterized by increased and healthy specialization. At last, now that Blake has escaped the status of a cult figure, scholars are able to work systematically at the details of his myth and the particulars of his sources. The critical work of S. Foster Damon, Northrop Frye, David Erdman, Harold Bloom, and several others has given us a Blake that we recognize as a major poet and whom we begin to understand. The textual, bibliographical, and biographical work of Geoffrey Keynes, David Erdman, G. E. Bentley, Jr., and others has provided trustworthy apparatus for scholarship and has shed a little light on an obscure life. Specialized work can now be carried forward confidently; and, at the same time, a book like this one can be written with fewer trepidations. Blake scholars will no doubt dispute many of my readings of individual poems and passages — many of the readings are indeed new — but they will recognize that I am writing about the same William Blake that the scholarship of the last fifty years has identified for us.

My brief account of Blake's life, heavily indebted to the excellent *Blake Records* of G. E. Bentley, Jr., is put forward in an attempt to provide as accurate a context for Blake's work as possible while sticking to the sparse facts. The remainder of the book is an account of Blake's opinions on life, eternity, art, and vision that is carried out by means of a survey of his writings that is usually chronological. But a significant exception to this type of organization is *The Book of Urizen* which is discussed somewhat earlier in the book than its date would justify because its brief treatment of Blake's major themes gives it special value as an introduction to Blake's thought and art. Because of Blake's reputation for obscurity, I make extensive use of quotation both to explicate the lines and to demonstrate that Blake can speak very well for himself. The William Blake who emerges from this study is an opponent of rational theology but an advocate of visionary Christianity; he is an uncompromising supporter of freedom from all institutions, laws, and moral codes; he is a Christian anarchist who is highly successful in finding myth and method, both to communicate his objections to our psychological bondage and to show us the perfect liberty to which unchained Imagination and Energy can lead us.

A Note on the Texts

For the convenience of the general reader, quotations from Blake's poetry and prose are based on *The Complete Writings of William Blake,* ed. Geoffrey Keynes (London: Oxford University Press, 1966), the text used in most Blake criticism and scholarship, including such reader's aids as *A Blake Dictionary.* Many Blake scholars feel that David Erdman's edition of *The Poetry and Prose of William Blake* should be regarded as the standard text, but the Keynes edition has its virtues and should remain, indefinitely, an alternative "standard" edition. Page numbers in the Keynes edition are given after all set-off quotations from Blake (e.g., K 227) and after many of the quotations that are integrated into the body of the discussion. Occasionally, in the interests of a less cluttered presentation, page references are omitted after short quotations that seem easy to locate because of the context of the discussion.

VICTOR N. PAANANEN

Michigan State University

Acknowledgments

I wish to thank Michigan State University for assignment to research duties in the summer of 1972, and for an All-University Research Grant that has helped with expenses in the production of a typescript. The Michigan State University Library and the London Library, St. James's Square, have generously provided books and a place to work on projects related to the subject of this book.

I have already suggested the indebtedness of this book to previous Blake scholarship. I wish to acknowledge further the general indebtedness of any critical work that I undertake to Professor Karl Kroeber, now at Columbia University, but whose courses at the University of Wisconsin were not only brilliant expositions of the literature and civilization of nineteenth-century England but also stimulating demonstrations of new possibilities for the criticism of imaginative literature. To my wife Donna I owe my mental and corporeal survival in the years that we have devoted to the academic life.

Chronology

1757   William Blake born November 28 at 28 Broad Street, London, son of James Blake, a shopkeeper. Baptized December 11 in St. James's Church, Piccadilly.

c. 1765 -
1767   Sees "a tree filled with angels" on Peckham Rye.

1772 -
1779   Apprenticed to James Basire, engraver. Probably lives with Basire's family at 31 Great Queen Street, Lincoln's Inn Fields. In 1774, begins sketching memorials in Westminster Abbey for Basire.

1779   October. Admitted as a student to the Royal Academy of Arts.

1780   June 6. Unwillingly caught in a mob storming Newgate Prison during anti-Catholic riots.

1782   August 18. Married to Catherine Boucher in St. Mary's Church, Battersea.

1783   Printing of *Poetical Sketches* arranged by John Flaxman and the Reverend and Mrs. Anthony Stephen Mathew.

1784   After his father's death in July, opens a printshop in partnership with James Parker, another former apprentice of James Basire.

1787   Death of his brother Robert, aged nineteen. Sees Robert's spirit rise to heaven, "clapping its hands for joy." Subsequently, Robert reveals method of Illuminated Printing to him in a dream.

1788   Publishes *There Is No Natural Religion* and *All Religions Are One*.

1789   April 13. Signs list of thirty-two resolutions passed at a founding convention of a New Church based on the teachings of Emanuel Swedenborg. Engraves and publishes *Songs of Innocence* and *Book of Thel*. About this time writes, but does not engrave or publish, *Tiriel*.

1790   Writing *The Marriage of Heaven and Hell.*

1791   *The French Revolution* prepared for the press but not printed.

1793   Prospectus offers *America, Visions of the Daughters of Albion, Thel, The Marriage of Heaven and Hell, Songs of Innocence, Songs of Experience.*

1794   Publishes *Songs of Innocence and of Experience, Europe, Book of Urizen.*

1795   Publishes *Book of Ahania, Book of Los,* and *Song of Los.*

1796   Illustrates Edward Young's *Night Thoughts.*

1797   At work on *Vala* (subsequently *The Four Zoas*).

1800   Takes cottage at Felpham made available by William Hayley.

1803   Forced to evict a soldier named Scolfield from his garden at Felpham. Scolfield brings charges of sedition. Returns to London to 17 South Moulton Street.

1804   Blake tried and acquitted at Chichester. Starts *Milton* (published 1809–10) and *Jerusalem* (published 1818–20). Visits Truchsessian Gallery.

1808   Edition of Robert Blair's *Grave*, illustrated by Blake, published.

1809   Exhibits paintings at 28 Broad Street and writes *Descriptive Catalogue*. Exhibition attacked by Robert Hunt in the *Examiner* as "fresh proof of the alarming increase of the effects of insanity."

1815 - 1818   Engraves for Wedgwood catalogues.

1816   Illustrates John Milton's "L'Allegro" and "Il Penseroso."

1821   Moves to Fountain Court, Strand.

1824   Illustrates John Bunyan's *Pilgrim's Progress.*

1826   Publishes his *Illustrations to the Book of Job.*

1827   At work on illustrations of Dante's *Divine Comedy* until his death on August 12. Buried in Bunhill Fields Burying Ground, the Dissenters' cemetery, but with the rites of the Church of England.

CHAPTER 1

Life and Times

BECAUSE very little is known about the life of William Blake, conjecture has often supplied the place of fact in the writing of his biography. The few authentic accounts that we have of Blake[1] picture a life of hard work and frequent disappointment, indeed of poverty and obscurity, that he faced with stout courage and unfailing cheerfulness. There is so little in the records to satisfy any sentimental notion of what we would have our inspired — or mad — poet be that we conclude that the real truths are yet to be found. Conversely, the intellectual movements that touched Blake in eighteenth-century London, and perhaps found their synthesis in him, seem to be too many and too confusedly entwined to satisfy our scrutiny any more than the biographical details do. We know that Blake's friends were Deists and Swedenborgians, Unitarians and Anglicans — but Blake himself can be found to be critical of aspects of each of these positions, at least from time to time.

If we seek less evident components in Blake's intellectual milieu — the Neo-Platonism of Thomas Taylor, the mysticism of Jacob Boehme, or the alchemical philosophy of Paracelsus — we have to admit to a quite disappointing degree of correspondence between what Blake has to say and what any one of these men had said. No one influence of the several possible influences on Blake serves to explain Blake's thought — not that the thought of an independent and creative thinker can ever be so explained — but, taken together, they form the rich context out of which Blake's work took shape. This philosophic context serves, in fact, as the source of all British Romantic thought; for William Wordsworth, Samuel Taylor Coleridge, and even Percy Shelley emerge from the same intellectual milieu, despite the wide divergences in outlook that exist among them and between each of them and Blake. Like the other British

Romantic poets, Blake found himself in an era characterized by new attitudes and approaches in philosophy, theology, and politics.

I *The Evangelical Movement*

The complex synthesis which formed the Romantic intellectual climate is much the same as the synthesis of influences that had taken place in theology during the eighteenth century in what is called "the Evangelical Movement." Probably William Law (1686–1761), the author of *Christian Perfection* and *A Serious Call* who had himself been a disciple of Jacob Boehme, had been the greatest influence on men who would later be Evangelicals — or Methodists[2] or even Swedenborgians.[3] Law had helped to inculcate a new respect for emotion and "mysticism" in religion, and he had laid the basis for the attack on rational Deism that the Evangelical clergy would lead. Blake makes no secret of his admiration for Evangelicals like John Wesley and George Whitefield; and he defends "Methodists," members of the new sect formed by a group of Evangelicals driven from the Church of England. Indeed, there seems to be considerable merit in T. B. Shepherd's relatively casual observation that "the greatest poet of the Evangelical Revival was William Blake."[4] If nothing else, the background provided by an awareness of the progress of the Evangelical movement helps us recognize that many of Blake's ideas had analogues and "context" within his own age.

When William Blake was born on November 28, 1757, in a house on no longer fashionable Broad Street, the Evangelical movement in the Church of England was already moving toward the important position it would attain in the nineteenth century. "Every Christian under their scheme," Prime Minister William Gladstone wrote of the Evangelicals, "had personal dealings with his God and Saviour. The Inner Life was again acknowledged as a reality, and substituted for that bare, bald compromise between the seen and the unseen world which reduces the share of the 'far more exceeding and eternal' almost to *nil*."[5] Whether Evangelical impulses reached Blake through Anglican or Dissenting connections we cannot be sure. Blake was baptized into the Church of England at St. James's Church, Piccadilly, on December 11, two weeks after his birth. Blake's father may later have joined a Dissenting group,[6] but Blake's Anglican baptism, marriage, and burial all suggest that Blake's allegiances were to the Church of England and not to Dissent.[7]

Still, whatever the source of Blake's introduction to visionary religion, we do know that between the ages of eight and ten he had rejected the "compromise between the seen and the unseen" with which most men of the preceding age had been contented:

On Peckham Rye (by Dulwich Hill) it is, as he will in after years relate, that while quite a child, of eight or ten perhaps, he had his "first vision." Sauntering along, the boy looks up and sees a tree filled with angels, bright angelic wings bespangling every bough like stars. Returned home he relates the incident, and only through his mother's intercession escapes a thrashing from his honest father, for telling a lie. Another time, one summer morn, he sees the haymakers at work, and amid them angelic figures walking.[8]

To see "angels" in this fashion is, in Gladstone's phrase, to acknowledge "the Inner Life" as "a reality." Blake was to argue forcefully in *There Is No Natural Religion* and elsewhere for the superiority of this mode of perception over the "compromise" of what he terms "ratio" vision.

Blake's boyhood circumstances were humble but not poverty-stricken ones thanks to his father's prospering shop. Blake's politics were generally those of his class in London — the class of shopkeepers and artisans — and thus Blake was always a "Liberty Boy." He would join Dissenters and Deists in supporting the French Revolution when it came; and he did so not only for reasons of class but because he clearly saw how poverty, vice, and civic brutality were perpetuated by both church and state. Indeed, as Stanley Gardner has effectively demonstrated, every social evil of the age was fully visible within yards of Blake's boyhood home.[9] He would attack many of the institutionally supported horrors of the era in some of the most destructively analytic poems in his *Songs of Experience.* But, in the meantime, he had to meet the obligations of his class; and, having first attended a drawing school, he was apprenticed to James Basire, an engraver.

From Basire, Blake learned the trade that sustained him, perhaps not very well at times, for the rest of his life. Assigned to sketch the monuments in Westminster Abbey, Blake developed rapidly as an artist; but the isolation and the silence of the Abbey freed him to attend to the reality of his Inner Life again: "It was when he was one day thus secluded in the dim vaulted solitude of Westminster Abbey that he saw, as he afterwards records, one of his visions. The aisles and galleries of the old building (or sanctuary) suddenly filled with a great procession of monks and priests, choristers and censer-bearers, and his entranced ear heard the chant of plain-song and chorale,

while the vaulted roof trembled to the sound of music."[10] The source
of Blake's art was never to be the external world or the models
provided by other men's work; instead, his source was always to be
his own Vision; and, in the incident in the Abbey, it allowed him to
see the living meaning of the structure rather than the dead stone
that he had been assigned to sketch.

II   *The Determination of Personal and Social Roles*

By October, 1779, when Blake was admitted as a student to the
Royal Academy of Art, it was already too late for him to accept the
artistic practice or habits of mind of the preceding age, Blake's
encounter with Sir Joshua Reynolds, the President of the Academy
and the great painter of the late eighteenth century, demonstrates
this fundamental aversion to Neo-Classical caution and precision:
" 'Once I remember his talking to me of Reynolds,' writes a surviving friend: 'he became furious at what the latter had dared to say of
his early works. When a very young man he had called on Reynolds
to show him some designs, and had been recommended to work with
less extravagance and more simplicity, and to correct his drawing.
This Blake seemed to regard as an affront never to be forgotten.' "[11]
Reynolds's recommendations for the checking of enthusiasm and
for the submission to compromises helped to make Reynolds serve as
Blake's model for the very enemy of Inspiration: "Reynolds's Opinion was that Genius May be Taught & that all Pretence to Inspiration is a Lie & a Deceit, to say the least of it. For if it is a Deceit, the
whole Bible is Madness" (K 452). Or, more directly, Blake's view of
Reynolds was that "This Man was Hired to Depress Art" (K 445).
Blake's inability to work to the standards of a Reynolds was to be one
major reason for his lack of a public as an artist — and as a poet —
for the rest of his life.
In Blake's responses to Reynolds over the years — primarily expressed in marginal comments to Reynolds's writings — there are
hints of another sort of feeling engendered by Blake's contact with
the Royal Academy and the "official" artists. Blake sees Reynolds as
willing to "Serve Nobility & Fashionable Taste"; and he argues that
Albert Dürer, an artist Blake admired deeply, "would never have got
his Manners from the Nobility" (K 940). These feelings remind us
again of Blake's political sympathies, despite our lack of specific
knowledge of any political activity on his part in these years other
than his being caught up by a mob storming Newgate Prison during
the Gordon riots directed against the Roman Catholics in 1780:

On . . . Tuesday, 6th of June, "the Mass-houses" having already been demolished — one, in Blake's near neighborhood, Warwick Street, Golden Square — and various private houses also; the rioters, flushed with gin and victory, were turning their attention to grander schemes of devastation. That evening, the artist happened to be walking in a route chosen by one of the mobs at large, whose course lay from Justice Hyde's house near Leicester Fields, for the destruction of which less than an hour had sufficed, through Long Acre, past the quiet house of Blake's old master, engraver Basire, in Great Queen Street, Lincoln's Inn Fields, and down Holborn, bound for Newgate. Suddenly, he encountered the advancing wave of triumphant Blackguardism, and was forced (for from such a great surging mob there is no disentanglement) to go along in the very front rank, and witness the storm and burning of the fortress-like prison, and release of its three hundred inmates.[12]

Although this event provides us with a vivid picture of the volatile character of the times, it has little value for an understanding of William Blake's own political views. Perhaps more insight into Blake's class origins, and therefore into his political perspective, can be found in his choice of a bride.

After an unsuccessful courtship of "a lively little girl" named Polly Wood, Blake met Catherine Boucher, who, we are told, pitied him because of his recent amatory disappointment and thus won his heart. Catherine, the daughter of a market gardener in Battersea, signed the marriage register with an "X," presumably because she was illiterate. And Catherine's circumstances, "respectable and industrious" but by no means fashionable, are a useful reminder that Blake's world was not that of the Royal Academy and official art (even though he would continue to have a few contacts with the Academy, some of them valuable). In any case, now that legends that so long surrounded Catherine have been cleared away, we can let a nearly contemporary tribute to her character stand:

Catherine . . . was endowed with a loving loyal nature, an adaptive open mind, capable of profiting by good teaching, and of enabling her, under constant high influence, to become a meet companion to her imaginative husband in his solitary and wayward course. Uncomplainingly and helpfully, she shared the low and rugged fortunes which over-originality ensured as his unvarying lot in life. She had mind and the ambition which follows. Not only did she prove a good housewife on straitened means, but in after-years, under his tuition and hourly companionship, she acquired, besides the useful arts of reading and writing, that which very few uneducated women with the honestest effort ever succeeded in attaining: some footing of equality with her husband. She, in time, came to work off his engravings as though she had been bred to the trade; nay, imbibed enough of his very own spirit to reflect it in Design which might almost have been his own.[13]

When we recall the suffering for both parties that characterized the marriages of S. T. Coleridge, Lord Byron, and Percy Shelley, we see readily that Blake was perhaps the one great Romantic poet who had found a wife who complemented — and perhaps even comprehended — his genius. And Blake found such a wife in the "illiterate daughter of a Battersea market-gardener."[14]

Although Blake's central concern through his period of apprenticeship and during his time at the Royal Academy would necessarily be his drawing, painting, and engraving, he did produce some poetry during his adolescence and young manhood. Many of the efforts were songs, sometimes fairly conventional but often charming ones, that Blake is known to have sung to music of his own composition. As Martin K. Nurmi has shown, much of the metrical innovation that readers see in these early songs and in Blake's later lyrics is in fact the result of Blake's first writing verse with music in mind. Blake, Nurmi explains, "had no interest in regular metres unless they served the musical effects he wanted, and he had the confidence to trust his own ear as to what these should be." Often, "Musical and verbal rhythms pull against each other . . . to create a rhythmical tension. . . ."[15] In addition to writing songs, Blake offered his responses to the poetic fashions of the age in ballad imitations ("Gwin, King of Norway" and "Fair Elenor"), in a fragment of pseudo-Elizabethan play ("King Edward the Third"), and in Ossianic prose poems.

Today, many of these productions remain of considerable interest because of their hints of the ideas and the methods that the mature Blake employed. In them we see Blake moving toward the creation of his later mythic figures in personifications of the seasons (influenced by James Thomson) and in Biblical and historical characters made to carry symbolic weight. To Samuel C. Chew, the Gothic verse narrative "Fair Elenor" reveals "an impassioned intensity beyond the capabilities of any Gothicizer,"[16] and Chew's remark reminds us that each of Blake's imitative works in eighteenth-century modes possesses his characteristic energy. Indeed, these experiments, when considered with the songs, stand as proof that Blake might well rank as the greatest of "pre-Romantic" poets did we not know that he eventually became a major Romantic poet. For the preservation of these works we are indebted to Blake's friends:

the Reverend A. S. Mathew, the clergyman of Percy Chapel and the afternoon preacher at St. Martin's-in-the-Fields; Harriet Mathew, his wife; and John Flaxman, the sculptor, who arranged the printing of these pieces as *Poetical Sketches* (1783) "By W. B."

Although the exact constitution of these social gatherings remains unknown, Blake seems to have met with friends like the Mathews and Flaxman for evenings like the one recorded in the unpublished satiric piece *An Island in the Moon* (which Blake must have written about 1784–85, perhaps to be read at an occasion such as he describes in it). Whoever the models for the characters were, the satire is notable for its attacks on what Blake later called "the Idiot Questioner" by characters called "the Antiquarian" and "Obtuse Angle" (the latter often identified as Mathew):

"Reason, Sir?" said the Antiquarian. "I'll give you an example for your reason. As I was walking along the street I saw a vast number of swallows on the rails of an old Gothic square. They seem'd to be going on their passage, as Pliny says. As I was looking up, a little *outré* fellow, pulling me by the sleeve, cries, 'Pray, Sir, who do all they belong to?' I turn'd myself about with great contempt. Said I, 'Go along, you fool!' 'Fool!' said he, 'who do you call fool? I only as'd you a civil question.' I had a great mind to have thrash'd the fellow, only he was bigger than I." (K 45)

Here, and in Obtuse Angle's later denunciation of "Queries," it is not too far-fetched to see the contempt for rational attempts to find truth ("Idiot Questioning," to Blake) that was to be found in many of Blake's subsequent utterances.

The gathering in *An Island in the Moon* contains, as Blake's own social circle probably did, such eighteenth-century types as the scientific virtuoso ("Inflammable Gass the Wind-finder") and the Antiquarian. And an enthusiastic preacher is described: " 'Ah, Mr. Huffcap would kick the bottom of the Pulpit out with Passion — would tear off the sleeve of his Gown & set his wig on fire & throw it at the people. He'd cry & stamp & kick & sweat, and all for the good of their souls' " (K 48). Mr. Huffcap is admired by a good Evangelical or Dissenting lady named Mrs. Sistagatist: " 'Oh!' said Mrs. Sistagatist. 'If it was not for churches & chapels I should not have liv'd so long. There was I, up in a Morning at four o'clock, when I was a Girl. I would run like the dickins till I was all in a heat. I would stand till I was ready to sink into the earth' " (K 48).

Blake himself is present as Quid the Cynic, and he drops hints about his methods as an engraver. (Flaxman is there too, many readers feel, as "Steelyard the Lawgiver.") But the most interesting feature of the work for most readers is the inclusion of the first draft of Blake's fine poem "Holy Thursday" which is offered as a song — and without irony[17] — by Obtuse Angle. Included as well are early versions of "Nurse's Song" and "The Little Boy Lost" which are used to evoke the powerful moods of childhood and thereby to create "good humour." (All three poems were later published in *Songs of Innocence.*)

Receiving a small inheritance resulting from his father's death in July, 1784, Blake seemed willing to try the life of the small shopkeeper into which he had been born. With James Parker, another former apprentice of James Basire, Blake opened a small printshop next door to the house of his birth on Broad Street. As was the case with any attempt that Blake made to serve "fashion," the enterprise did not succeed; but this was the period of Blake's valuable association with his favorite brother, Robert Blake, a boy in his teens but already capable of sketches "characterized by Blake-like feeling and intention."[18] Robert was to die before he could fulfill his promise as an artist:

Blake affectionately tended him in his illness, and during the last fortnight of it watched continuously day and night by his bedside, without sleep. When all claim had ceased with that brother's last breath, his own exhaustion showed itself in an unbroken sleep of three days' and nights' duration. The mean room of sickness had been to the spiritual man, as to him most scenes were, a place of vision and revelation; for Heaven lay about him still, in manhood, as in infancy it "lies about us" all. At the last solemn moment, the visionary eyes beheld the released spirit ascend heavenward through the matter-of-fact ceiling, "clapping its hands for joy". . . .[19]

But it seems that the visionary eye that saw the significance of his brother's death would never lose touch with Robert's genius: "Down to late age the survivor talked much and often of that dear brother; and in hours of solitude and inspiration his form would appear and speak to the poet in consolatory dream, in warning or helpful vision."[20] Blake's characteristic method of illuminated printing, the method to be used to publish his poetry and its complementary illustration, was revealed to him by Robert in a dream: "In a vision of the night, the form of Robert stood before him . . . directing him to the technical mode by which could be produced a fac-simile of song and design."[21] The first of Blake's productions in this mode were to be his tractates in defense of Vision and Inspiration, *There Is No Natural Religion* and *All Religions Are One* (both 1788).

III *Swedenborgianism and Revolution*

In April, 1789, after Blake had made known his views about Deism and about perception in *There Is No Natural Religion* and *All Religions Are One*, Blake and his wife were drawn to a meeting held by readers of Swedenborg to discuss the founding of a New Church. Many Swedenborgians, most notably T. Hartley and John Clowes, the translators of Swedenborg's works into English, found it unnecessary to leave the Church of England; but the Swedenborgians who gathered at a public house on April 13, 1789, found that the existing churches were too deeply tainted by what Blake had already attacked as natural religion:

> The Old Church . . . believes that nature is God. . . .
> The Old Church faith should be abolished.
> While the Old Church lasts, Heaven cannot come to man.[22]

Although he would be writing against certain of Swedenborg's views within about a year, Blake signed the list of thirty-two resolutions passed at the meeting, as did Catherine.[23] It now seems that Blake's brief flirtation with the Swedenborgian New Church was a predictable result of his growing up with the Evangelical movement. In the determination of the assembled Swedenborgians to replace faith "directed to a God invisible and incomprehensible,"[24] the Evangelical need for "personal dealings with . . . God and Saviour" can be detected. And the visionary Swedenborg not only had valued the "Inner Life," to return to Gladstone's remark yet again, but had also constructed his own science of correspondences "between the seen and the unseen." But Blake was soon to discover Swedenborg's limits — his abhorrent views on predestination and his conventional moral notions — and thus refuse Swedenborg his discipleship.

The mere fact, however, that Swedenborg's appeal was so strong — and Blake's respect for him continued throughout his life — is another indication of Blake's participation and interest in the spirit of the time. London in this period abounded in visionary religions and in fads ranging from vegetarianism to nudism; but that Blake was never an enrolled disciple of even so rational a visionary as Emanuel Swedenborg, let alone of a Joanna Southcott (who promised to give birth to the Saviour — and drew Blake's friend William Sharp as a follower), is proof of his possession not only of a resistance to fads but also of an intellectual independence that was a necessary trait among men intrigued by the new possibilities of the early days of the Romantic period. From Swedenborg, Blake drew vocabulary and some concepts; but Blake was never one to be "enslav'd by another Man's" (K 629) system, no matter how much of the Inner Light it might have.

But 1789, the year of Blake's participation in the Swedenborgian meeting, was also the year that saw the initial polarization of views in response to the event that would most influence British intellectual and political life in the nineteenth century —the revolution in France. The Unitarian Dr. Richard Price gave a sermon in the Old Jewry that greeted the revolution as little short of the prelude to the Apocalypse ("I could almost say, 'Lord, now lettest thou thy servant depart in peace, for mine eyes have seen thy salvation.' . . . I have lived to see thirty millions of people, indignant and resolute, spurning at slavery, and demanding liberty with an irresistable voice."[25]). With Edmund Burke's reply in defense of the Old Order, there had been initiated the debate on the French Revolution that found Blake in the camp of the Deist Thomas Paine and the Atheist William Godwin.

Paine and Godwin were strange comrades-in-arms for Blake perhaps (and we know that Blake particularly detested Godwin), but we have no reason to think that Blake had anything in common with them beyond politics. Paine's *Rights of Man*, Godwin's *Political Justice*, and Blake's *French Revolution* (set up in proof and bearing the imprint of Joseph Johnson, but never published) were all replies to Burke in defense of the principles of the Revolution. As we shall subsequently see, Blake's treatment of the Revolution differs markedly from that of the others in his characteristically seeing its events as the beginning of a movement toward the perfect liberty that the return to Eternity represents to him.

IV Lambeth, Felpham, and the Treason Trial

After leaving the Broad Street shop, the Blakes lived from 1785 to 1790 in Poland Street and then from 1790 to 1800 at 13 Hercules Buildings, Lambeth, in the neighborhood of Lambeth Palace. Blake had already written the *Songs of Innocence*, demonstrating the transforming power the innocent eye possesses, before moving from Poland Street, but he produced in Lambeth almost all of the writings for which he is best known, with the exception of *Milton* and *Jerusalem.* Here he wrote the *Songs of Experience*, which, by revealing the institutional, moral, and mental restraints under which we exist, point the way to the Eternity that authenticates the innocent's intuitions. These poems he engraved, together with *Innocence,* as the fully coherent *Songs of Innocence and of Experience* (1794).

In the same year, he treated the psychological damage inflicted by a restrictive moral code in *Visions of the Daughters of Albion;* he gave the fall from the freedom of Eternity a mythic treatment in the *Book of Urizen;* and he continued his anatomy of that process in *The Book of Ahania* and *The Book of Los* in the following year. About 1796 he began a long struggle to give the psychological processes of this fall epic expression in *The Four Zoas,* called *Vala* in an earlier form, a work that he returned to from time to time until about 1807 but did not engrave. *Europe* (1794) was an even earlier try at the psychological themes of *The Four Zoas;* and *The Four Zoas* was itself to be Blake's quarry for materials to be used in the later epics *Milton* and *Jerusalem.*

In Lambeth, Blake had some success as an engraver and illustrator of the works of others, although his fine illustrations for Edward Young's *Night Thoughts* (1797) were not well received. But personal details are scarce for the Lambeth period, even as they are scarce for almost every period of Blake's life. What we see in such letters and contemporary references as do exist are once again largely the concerns of a trade and a class. Only Blake's writings themselves tell us much about the mental life of the man.

At the end of the Lambeth period, Blake acquired a patron, William Hayley; and the Blakes moved to a cottage at Felpham made available by Hayley, who lived nearby. But Hayley's fondness for "the good Enthusiastic Blake"[26] brought with it no understanding of Blake's goals as an artist and as a poet. Finally, in 1803, weary of his patron's "Genteel Ignorance & Polite Disapprobation" (K 825), Blake knew that he had to return to London. Before he could leave, however, there occurred the one dramatic event in Blake's corporeal life.

On August 12, 1802, Blake found a soldier named John Scolfield in his garden, probably invited there by a gardener but without Blake's knowledge; and Blake asked him to leave. Scolfield refused, became abusive, and forced Blake to push him from the garden and then fifty yards up the road to the inn where the soldiers were barracked. Scolfield had Blake brought to trial for sedition, alleging that Blake had "*damned the King & said the ——— Soldiers were all Slaves.*"[27] There can be no doubting that, whether Blake said what

Scolfield ascribed to him or not, Blake's republican sentiments would be accurately reflected in the remark; but, with the aid of an able attorney named Samuel Rose, Blake was acquitted when his case came to trial in January, 1804. The indictment itself is, however, a vivid reminder of the times in which Blake lived. The fears engendered by the events of the French Revolution had cost Englishmen many of their traditional liberties and had produced networks of government spies: apparently the soldier Scolfield sought to take advantage of the temper of the times to sooth his wounded pride.

V *The Unregarded Prophet*

When Blake had again settled down to work in London, his freedom from Hayley's interference and his exhilaration at escaping Scolfield's net led to a burst of creativity that included his starting work on *Milton* and *Jerusalem*, but the completion of either was to be years away. He felt, he said after a visit to a collection of pictures exhibited by Joseph, Count Truchsess, "enlightened with the light I enjoyed in my youth," adding "I am really drunk with intellectual vision" (K 852). Blake continued, however, to meet with every sort of frustration in his own work as a painter and an engraver. Symptomatic of his experiences in the later years was his attempt to gain some recognition — and to interest the public in his idea of portable frescoes that could be changed from time to time in England's public buildings — by holding an exhibition of his work at 28 Broad Street, the place of his birth and now the hosiery shop of his brother James.

Although Blake displayed works that are now priceless and that are in the great museums and private collections of the world, and although he offered as a guidebook to the exhibition the sourcebook of his ideas, *The Descriptive Catalogue*, he had small success with the show. But, worst of all, was the response of the exhibition's one reviewer, Robert Hunt, who regarded Blake's efforts as "fresh proof of the alarming increase of the effects of insanity."[28] Hunt had attacked Blake's work before, probably because, as G. E. Bentley, Jr., observes, he "saw him as an enthusiast, if not a Methodist."[29] But that the one public voice raised by Blake's exhibition should be that of an old enemy could only confirm Blake in his decision to accept henceforth his obscurity. Indeed, Blake had already said of himself, "I am hid" (K 445)

The years that followed the exhibition of 1809 brought Blake's then unrecognized crowning achievements: the publication of *The Illustrations to the Book of Job* (1826) and the completion in illuminated printing of *Milton* (c. 1810) and of *Jerusalem* (c. 1820). These epic works invited England to embrace a new theology that was based not on a restrictive moral code but on the forgiveness of sins and that had its source in the Imagination, which was Jesus present in every man. For those who wished to see Blake as their favorite madman, as H. Crabb Robinson wished to see him, he was willing to veil his comments on Vision in a way calculated to entertain his auditor. We now see Blake's conversations with Robinson for the complex teasing of the naive interrogator that they really are.[30] At least Blake had Catherine's company and understanding, and he had also passed beyond wanting material success:

> I have Mental Joy & Mental Health
> And Mental Friends & Mental wealth;
> I've a Wife I love & that loves me;
> I've all But Riches Bodily.
> I am in God's presence night & day,
> And he never turns his face away. (K 558)

Blake also had not only the patronage of Thomas Butts that was limited only by his limited means but the admiration of a few fellow artists to sustain him in the final period of his life.

Blake's last years seem to have been peaceful and cheerful and to have been made that way by his certainty of the truth of his vision and by his awareness of what he had indeed accomplished in his art despite lack of recognition. His attitude as he was dying on August 12, 1827, is only in character: "Just before he died his Countenance became fair, his eyes brighten'd, and he burst out into singing of the things he saw in heaven."[31] Because he had "ever professed his preference of the Church to any sort of sectarianism,"[32] Blake asked for burial in the Church of England: "A little before his death, Mrs. Blake asked where he would be buried, and whether a dissenting minister or a clergyman of the Church of England should read the service. To which he answered that 'as far as his own feelings were concerned, they might bury him where she pleased.' But that as 'father, mother, aunt, and brother were buried in Bunhill-row, perhaps it would be better to lie *there*. As to service, he should wish for that of the Church of England.'"[33] Catherine Blake followed him to Bunhill Fields on October 20, 1831; but this "estimable woman . . . saw Blake frequently after his decease: he used to come and sit with her two or three hours every day."[34] Clearly, Catherine Blake had learned from William the ability to see "through the eye and not with it" — to prefer what the Imagination sees to that which the rational mind tells us we must see — the same preference that Blake's genius may yet teach much of mankind.

CHAPTER 2

Poetry and Perception: The Two Tracts on Religion and The Book of Urizen

I *Poetry in Illuminated Printing*

Allegory address'd to the Intellectual powers, while it is altogether hidden from the Corporeal Understanding, is My Definition of the Most Sublime Poetry.

—Letter to Thomas Butts, July 6, 1803 (K 825)

If the Spectator could Enter into these Images in his Imagination, approaching them on the Fiery Chariot of his Contemplative Thought . . . then would he arise from his Grave, then would he meet the Lord in the Air & then he would be happy.

—*A Vision of the Last Judgment* (K 611)

THE works that William Blake offered to the unreceptive public of his day are a unique combination of the arts of printmaking and of poetry. In works like *The Book of Urizen* or *Visions of the Daughters of Albion,* each page contains both a portion of the poem's text — in many cases, only a few lines — and a fully colored engraved drawing that either illustrates the text or otherwise complements it. (There are also full-page illustrations between pages with text.) Some of Blake's poems survive in forms other than that represented by the engraved works — *Poetical Sketches* was printed in the conventional manner as an unillustrated book of poems; *The French Revolution* exists only in the form of the publisher's proof sheets and lacks illustration; and several poems, including the magnificent *Four Zoas,* were left in manuscript by Blake and not engraved.

Works like these can be represented in print with varying degrees of accuracy, as can Blake's letters and miscellaneous prose. But the character of the engraved works, to which Blake's greatest efforts were devoted, cannot be represented accurately in any conventional printed text. In fact, it has only recently been technically possible to produce first-rate color reproductions of the engraved work; and every serious student of Blake should make the effort to examine the Trianon Press facsimiles of Blake's poems published by the William Blake Trust under the guidance of Sir Geoffrey Keynes. Yet few readers can see these editions except in the rare-book rooms of libraries; for the actual appearance of Blake's pages remains unavailable as we read his poems in printed editions or in cheaper black-and-white facsimiles. Perhaps, however, colored slides of the Trianon facsimiles, or cheap reprints of them, will some day become widely available and thereby overcome the present difficulty of access to Blake's engraved work.

In producing a work in Illuminated Printing, Blake wrote the lines of his poem and drew the accompanying pictures on copper plates. He used acid to etch the areas of the plate surrounding his lettering and the lines of his drawing. The result was a plate that could be used in printing at least the all-important outlines of his work. Blake still had to color the reproduced page by hand, varying the colors from one copy to the next, and often shifting the order of the plates.[1] The fact that the sequence of plates could be changed is one of the unique characteristics of Blake's methods as a narrative poet. It suggests that the individual plates have greater significance in themselves than has the overall narrative ordering of the poem. To understand what led Blake to value the plate above sequential narrative, we must turn to two early prose tracts that also serve as a fine introduction to Blake's thought.

II   There Is No Natural Religion *and* All Religions Are One

In *There Is No Natural Religion* (1788), Blake's opposition to the dominant British empirical school of philosophy is made known. The reliance on sense experience that had characterized the thought of John Locke and the respect for experiment that had started in England with Francis Bacon had led in the eighteenth century to a philosophy that admitted no truth from sources other than our sense experiences and our reasonings based upon them. The result of this attitude was the assertion that there exists a "natural religion," a system of religious belief identifiable by means of the senses and logic.

For William Blake, "There Is No Natural Religion" because the theory of knowledge that supports such systems produces not insight into divinity but awareness of our enclosure within an inhuman circle. In *There Is No Natural Religion* (first series, written in 1788), Blake argues that, if we have knowledge only from the senses, we can only identify "objects of sense" as what we desire:

Man's desires are limited by his perceptions, none can desire what he has not perceiv'd.
The desires & perceptions of man, untaught by any thing but organs of sense, must be limited to objects of sense. (K 97)

How can sense experience produce religious knowledge, Blake asks, when sense experience does not even lead us to *ask* for religious knowledge? All that "sense" produces is an enclosed, inhuman world: "*Conclusion.* If it were not for the Poetic or Prophetic character the Philosophic & Experimental would soon be at the ratio of all things, & stand still, unable to do other than repeat the same dull round over again" (K 97).

Sense experience leads us to an acceptance of *ratio,* the lowest common denominator picture of the world that "common sense" takes for granted. Such a world offers no hint of possible divinity, and no moral guidance either. But, since there is another faculty in man, man is not "only a natural organ subject to Sense"; he possesses what Blake here calls the Poetic or Prophetic Character and what he elsewhere calls the Poetic Genius or the Imagination. As Blake explains later in his commentary on his lost painting *The Vision of the Last Judgment,* he personally rejects the "ratio" way of perceiving for the Poetic and Imaginative: "'What,' it will be Question'd, 'When the Sun rises, do you not see a round disk of fire somewhat like a Guinea?' O no, no, I see an Innumerable company of the Heavenly host crying 'Holy, Holy, Holy is the Lord God Almighty.' I question not my Corporeal or Vegetative Eye any more than I would Question a Window concerning a Sight. I look thro' it & not with it" (K 617). What man perceives as a "natural organ subject to Sense" is of no more interest than is the window that we look out of: what we must attend to is what the Imagination sees. Until we learn to value imaginative perception above "natural" perception, we receive no information at all about what is really important to man.

In *There Is No Natural Religion* (second series, probably also written in 1788), Blake turns from an attack on eighteenth-century empiricism to an assertion of the powers of the Imagination by which man "perceives more than sense (tho' ever so acute) can discover." Because empiricism allows itself only the world of the senses, it condemns itself to imprisonment in the physical world: "The bounded is loathed by its possessor. The same dull round, even of a universe, would soon become a mill with complicated wheels" (K 97). We are trapped, our senses say, in a mill — a grim, revolving machine in which the planets spin coldly in complicated circles. This is the universe that we choose, even though "the bounded is loathed by its possessor," when we accept "ratio" perception. And what we see is really ourselves since we acquiesce in what the universe seems to be: "*Application.* He who sees the Infinite in all things, sees God. He who sees the Ratio only, sees himself only" (K 98).

In the acts of the Imagination, however, "God becomes as we are" because the Imagination is Divine. If we will be imaginative, rather than ratio-bound, then "we may be as [God] is." God exists not in the natural world to which natural religionists apply their reason but in each of us and in the Imagination itself. "This world of Imagination," Blake writes elsewhere, "is the world of Eternity; it is the divine bosom into which we shall all go after the death of the Vegetated body" (K 605). In fact, even the natural world itself is, in a way, an imaginative creation, although we have frozen it into the cold mill that the ratio sees: "All Things are comprehended in their Eternal Forms in . . . the Human Imagination" (K 605–06). But the Imagination is also "the divine body of the Saviour, the true Vine of Eternity" (K 606). The healthy human Imagination *is* Jesus. When our perception becomes fully imaginative, the mill-universe ceases to imprison us, and we are once again with Him in Eternity.

In *All Religions Are One*, Blake again argues that all religious knowledge comes, of course, from the Divine imaginative faculty, "The true Man is the source, he being the Poetic Genius." The "true Man," the real man, is any imaginative human being who has freed himself from the bounded universe of the senses and is thus free to offer prophecy from the Imagination: "*Principle 1st.* That the Poetic Genius is the true Man, and that the body or outward form of Man is derived from the Poetic Genius" (K 98). Our perception of our own bodies, like our perception of the universe, is the acceptance of a frozen imaginative act. Similarly, every religion is an authentic imaginative creation distorted only by whatever each prophet has permitted to limit his vision — such as the character of the physical world that he thinks he inhabits or the nature of his civilization. Thus, all religions *are* one because they "have one source," the Divine and eternal Imagination.

III   *The Characteristics of Blake's Visionary Mode in Poetry*

Because Blake believes that our "natural" perception would only deceive and entrap us but that our imaginative perception can bring us truth and freedom, he tries in all his work as a poet and a painter to give us a world seen not *with* the eye but *through* it. One effect of his attempt to offer imaginative Vision rather than natural sight is, paradoxically perhaps, a radical simplification of his materials down to what communicates his vision and pays no homage to the deceptive natural world. As a result, conventional landscape all but disappears in his poetry, as do "realistically" portrayed human beings. Whether the poem is a Song of Innocence or *Jerusalem*, "simplification," in this sense, is present; for, as Harold Bloom says, Blake's poems ".refuse to seek the visually remembered world."[2] Nonetheless, precisely this sort of simplicity has made Blake hard for many readers to comprehend, but it is the appropriate mode for a poet who tries to lead us to truths knowable not by sense experience but by the Poetic Genius or Imagination.

Blake's own remarks about art stress the importance of clear "outline" in painting. The true artist is not interested in reproducing the natural world, the world of the senses, but in communicating his vision by means of sharp, clear lines. In this way, the painter simplifies, as does the poet, by ignoring what the senses allow us to see instead of what *is* real — what is imaginative.

Complaints of Blake's "obscurity" were common even in his own day, but Blake's answer to one such indictment should settle the issue once and for all: "You say that I want somebody to Elucidate my Ideas. But you ought to know that What is Grand is necessarily obscure to Weak men. That which can be made Explicit to the Idiot is not worth my care. The wisest of the Ancients consider'd what is not too Explicit as the fittest for Instruction, because it rouzes the faculties to act" (K 793). Blake's poetry and his drawings are instruction in Vision. Their existence "rouzes the faculties to act" because they are addressed to "the intellectual powers" and not to "the corporeal understanding" that needs, even in art, a recognizable natural world as a crutch. Blake invites us to make the effort to share his vision as it exists in its radical, imaginative simplicity.

Since the source of Blake's vision is the eternal Imagination, he holds out the promise that, when he pictures Eternity, we can arise from the "grave" of our lives and "be happy" if we can "enter into these images." But most often Blake's visionary simplicity is instead applied to letting us see the truth of our present but mistaken mental states. Blake, looking *through* the eye and not *with* it, sees into our condition and reduces it to the meaningful, clear outlines that he then addresses to our "intellectual powers." To achieve these descriptions of perception, fallen or fulfilled, Blake uses the plate as his unit. Unlike traditional narratives, his epic poems reveal their patterns of meaning not exclusively at the end but constantly, plate by plate.[3]

As Northrop Frye says, in the conventional narrative, "theme" is "the narrative seen as total design"; but in Blake's work there is an "elimination of narrative movement" and "the device of a sequence of plates is consistent with the whole scheme."[4] The plates can in fact be shifted without great concern for a narrative structure. As S. Foster Damon has said of Blake's shifting plates in *The Book of Urizen*, "the 'states' which they represent are eternal, and therefore continually happening everywhere."[5] Each plate represents a mode of Vision, good or bad; and it invites our intellectual powers to apprehend and evaluate it. If the reader of Blake keeps this fact in mind, he can overcome much of the frustration that some readers feel as a result of what they consider to be narrative confusion or repetition. Blake is writing epics without narrative, but they have significance that can be apprehended plate by plate as our modes of Vision encounter those that he depicts.

In defining modes of perception in the poetic portion of his plate, Blake turns to myth. He rarely, however, uses as Milton did, any conventional figures from Classical or Christian myth; he invents his own figures, particularly Urizen, Los, Orc, Albion, and others of considerable importance. The relationships between these figures have the same function as do any of Blake's drawings for his illuminated printing: they provide the clear outlines that define particular modes of Vision. The figures must be self-defining rather than traditionally identifiable because their function requires that they be apprehended immediately by our "intellectual powers" rather than identified through our use of memory or other aspects of the "corporeal understanding."

IV   The Book of Urizen

The best work to introduce the reader to Blake's mythic figures and narrative method is *The Book of Urizen* (1794), a work that is concerned most directly with the problem of the limits that we place on our perception in our acceptance of the natural world. The events in *The Book of Urizen* are a "history" that we re-enact every time that we look at the world and see the ratio rather than the infinite: it is Urizen's fall that we participate in daily with our unimaginative looking. However the plates are arranged,[6] our vision darkens as we move through *The Book of Urizen* to repeat the fall of the human imaginative powers.

The title page of *The Book of Urizen* pictures an old man, with what are apparently blind eyes, writing with both hands. Behind him stand the stone tablets of the Ten Commandments, and he is enclosed within a series of semi-circular forms. The old man is Urizen, whose book this is; and he is one of Blake's most important mythic figures. The name "Urizen" is undoubtedly a pun on "Your Reason," but many readers also find a hint of the word "horizon" with its suggestion of limitations set on vision or indeed of the Greek original of "horizon," οὑρίζειν, which means "to limit," an activity that is psychologically necessary to Urizen.[7]

But to know what Urizen is, it is best to let the poem define him. The poem's "Preludium" suggests that Urizen is "the primeval Priest" and the source of a "religion" that is spurned by the Eternals who dictate the poem to Blake. We recognize here that the word "Eternals" is simply another synonym for the Imagination, the source of all truth for Blake. Thus we know that Urizen's "religion," whatever it might be, is unimaginative and is, therefore, as suspect as is natural religion. But again we must let the poem speak for itself.

Chapter I begins with the appearance of an ominous force in Eternity:

> Lo, a shadow of horror is risen
> In Eternity! Unknown, unprolific,
> Self-clos'd, all-repelling: what Demon
> Hath form'd this abominable void,
> This soul-shuddering vacuum? Some said
> "It is Urizen." But unknown, abstracted,
> Brooding, secret, the dark power hid. (K 222)

We have no recognizable landscape because we are still in Eternity prior to the coming into existence of the limited physical world that we know. Only mental states are described because they are the source of our delusions about the kind of world we inhabit.

Urizen is mysterious, unproductive, and self-contemplating rather

than open and creative. From such mental states, which precede
what we call "the existence of matter," there arises the fundamental
error in our perception. The falling Urizen (like our falling perception) defines and accepts limits:

> Times on times he divided & measur'd
> Space by space in his ninefold darkness,
> Unseen, unknown. . . . (K 222)

Through his mental attitudes, we know Urizen best. He is "Your
Reason" in all its inadequacy — despite its presumption of primacy
in the makeup of man. He is the faculty that respects ratio.

"The Eye altering alters all" (K 426), Blake says elsewhere. And,
once Urizen's mental condition is made known, his angle of vision
defined, a "physical" world begins to find its troubled existence:

> changes appear'd
> Like desolate mountains, rifted furious
> By the black winds of perturbation.
>
> For he strove in battles dire,
> In unseen conflictions with shapes
> Bred from his forsaken wilderness
> Of beast, bird, fish, serpent & element,
> Combustion, blast, vapour and cloud.
>
> Dark, revolving in silent activity:
> Unseen in tormenting passions:
> An activity unknown and horrible,
> A self-contemplating shadow,
> In enormous labours occupied.
>
> But Eternals beheld his vast forests;
> Age on ages he lay, clos'd, unknown,
> Brooding shut in the deep; all avoid
> The petrific, abominable chaos. (K 222-23)

From the perspective of Eternity, the activity of Urizen is simply
proof that he has lost his mental health. As he begins "creation," he
in fact brings chaos into existence because chaos, properly understood, is a world frozen into physical form — deathlike, "petrific" —
rather than flexible as is Eternity. "Many suppose," Blake writes

elsewhere, "that before the Creation All was Solitude & Chaos. This is the most pernicious Idea that can enter the Mind . . ." (K 614). Eternity is an active and energetic place; chaos is the "created" world.

We see now why *The Book of Urizen* is called Blake's "Book of Genesis" by many readers. What Urizen is doing is acting as a creator God, but he does so only because of his diseased mental condition — "unprolific," "self-closed," "abstracted," "secret" — and he is that faculty in us that repeats this same false creative process every time we see a fixed physical world around us. Blake effectively communicates the horror of our condition with his adjectives "petrific" and "abominable" and in what follows:

> His cold horrors silent, dark Urizen
> Prepar'd; his ten thousands of thunders,
> Rang'd in gloom'd array, stretch out across
> The dread world; & the rolling of wheels,
> As of swelling seas, sound in his clouds,
> In his hills of stor'd snows, in his mountains
> Of hail & ice; voices of terror
> Are heard, like thunders of autumn
> When the cloud blazes over the harvests. (K 223)

Such horrors of physical existence as winter weather ("cold . . . stor'd snows . . . hail & ice"), as turbulent seas ("swelling seas"), and as preparations for war are suggested. And all these terrors are, in their origin, mental realities too — they are brought into being by Urizen's madness.

Chapter II of *The Book of Urizen* provides still more information about that aspect of our psychological composition that Urizen represents. Chapter I has made it clear that he is all that is uncreative and secretive in us and that he needs, therefore, a ratio world to lean on. He has chosen, the opening of Chapter II reminds us, the "dim rocks" of the created universe in place of the "all flexible senses" that unfallen man, the psychologically whole man, could have. But his madness grows as he ascribes divinity to his unprolific and unimaginative act:

> "From the depths of dark solitude, From
> The eternal abode in my holiness,
> Hidden, set apart, in my stern counsels,
> Reserv'd for the days of futurity,

> I have sought for a joy without pain,
> For a solid without fluctuation.
> Why will you die, O Eternals?
> Why live in unquenchable burnings?" (K 224)

With comic pomposity ("my holiness"), Urizen asumes the God-like
position which man has mistakenly granted the rational faculty.
Rather than the complex excitement and diversity of Eternity, he
wishes an impossible one-dimensional world with no pain, no flux,
no death, no passion; in fact, he desires an Eternity not unlike the
Heaven that rational Christianity has long envisioned. In the same
way that he has started the creation of the fixed physical world
"Where nothing was" by turning sickly inward to oppose the
creative diversity of Eternity ("First I fought with the fire, con-
sum'd/ Inwards into a deep world within:/ A void immense . . ."),
he now turns inward to find a rigid one-dimensional moral law:

> Here alone I, in books form'd of metals,
> Have written the secrets of wisdom,
> The secrets of dark contemplation. . . .
> . . . .
> Lo! I unfold my darkness, and on
> This rock place with strong hand the Book
> Of eternal brass, written in my solitude. . . . (K 224)

Already we have enough experience with Blake to suspect anything
that can be described as "secrets . . . secrets . . . dark" that are written in the unhealthy voluntary self-enclosure expressed in "alone . . .
my darkness . . . my solitude." Finally, Urizen's insanity results in
his assumption of the role of holy lawgiver:

> "Laws of peace, of love, of unity,
> Of pity, compassion, forgiveness;
> Let each chuse one habitation,
> His ancient infinite mansion,
> One command, one joy, one desire,
> One curse, one weight, one measure,
> One King, one God, one Law." (K 224)

As Urizen's madness grows into the frenzied chant "*One* command,
one . . . one . . . One . . . one . . . one . . . One . . . one . . . one,"
Blake's skillful presentation allows a characteristic grim humor to
emerge to aid us in recognizing and judging what we see. Even as

Urizen has been revealed as our concept of a creator-God ("I re-
pell'd/ The vast waves & arose on the waters. . . ."), he is also the
lawgiver God of Mount Sinai. Both pictures of God are entirely false,
Blake would say; they are the result of our worship of the Urizen-
faculty in our psychological makeup.

Because Urizen makes laws, he brings into existence, for the first
time, "All the seven deadly sins of the soul." Systems of "sin" are
one result of the sort of perception that demands fixity, a corollary to
the creation of our stony world, which continues to take place:

> Eternity roll'd wide apart,
> Wide asunder rolling;
> Mountainous all around
> Departing, departing, departing,
> Leaving ruinous fragments of life
> Hanging, frowning cliffs, & all between,
> An ocean of voidness unfathomable. (K 225)

Urizen tries to find a home in this world, but he cannot until he
creates the additional limits which are, because the result of *one* error, simultaneously our universe, our planet, *and* our skull:

> And a roof, vast, petrific, around
> On all sides he fram'd like a womb,
> Where thousands of rivers in veins
> Of blood pour down the mountains to cool
> The eternal fires, beating without
> From Eternals; & like a black globe,
> View'd by sons of Eternity standing
> On the shore of the infinite ocean,
> Like a human heart, strugling & beating,
> The vast world of Urizen appear'd. (K 225–26)

What Urizen has done is to "create" in a manner that satisfies,
perhaps, the rational faculty's craving for definites; but, in the
process, he has separated himself from the genuine imaginative
sources of truth. He has, in fact, repeated the process by which
British empirical philosophy created its own mill-universe, the
closed world that the mind first creates and then declares the only
source of knowledge.

The faculty in the human psychology that Urizen in his assumed
sovereignty has thrust aside is Imagination that is represented most
nearly in Blake's mythology by Los who has suffered the loss of Eter-

nity in Urizen's insane wish for restriction rather than for flexibility. Because all that we see is imaginative, the world that Urizen creates is also imaginative; but Urizen has frozen his world into a false fixity. Or, mythically speaking, he has forced Los to make the creation of Urizen seem permanent. With Urizen's choice of the enclosure which is our universe, "Eternity stood wide apart,/ As the stars are apart from the earth." The distance of the stars above our heads is immediate evidence of the fashion in which we as "perceivers" have lost possession of our "perception." In *The Four Zoas*, man begins his return to Eternity by reaching upward to pull down the moon and the stars. But in *Urizen* Los is forced, "cursing his lot," "to confine/ The obscure separation alone" — to confirm Urizen, and mankind, in diseased solipsism.

Urizen is "Unorganiz'd" in his demand for fixity because only in Eternity is there a healthy organization that would include a balance in the claims of the different mental faculties. Urizen creates "Death," as the Eternals point out, because he reduces mankind to the status of a "clod of clay." One of Blake's favorite ironies is that those whom we call "the living" are actually "the dead."

Forced to freeze the products of the Imagination, Los struggles in anguished darkness, working as a blacksmith to make permanent Urizen's changes. In the process, he creates time:

> The Eternal Prophet heav'd the dark bellows,
> And turn'd restless the tongs, and the hammer
> Incessant beat, forging chains new & new,
> Numb'ring with links hours, days & years. (K 227)

With each limitation, the human mind becomes less imaginative:

> Forgetfulness, dumbness, necessity,
> In chains of the mind locked up,
> Like fetters of ice shrinking together,
> Disorganiz'd, rent from Eternity,
> Los beat on his fetters of iron,
> And heated his furnaces, & pour'd
> Iron sodor and sodor of brass. (K 228)

As Los hammers out the limitations of man, the forms of our physical body emerge. The first part to appear is the head: "a roof, shaggy wild, inclos'd/ In an orb his fountain of thought" (K 228). The mental disorder of self-ordained enclosure, presented here in a manner almost comic, materializes into the particular head of a man. The spine, ribs, heart, and stomach follow; and the senses are reduced to the frail and deceptive instruments that we know.

Because our senses are so limited, we no longer have full, imaginative participation in Eternity. Instead, we possess the chaotic sea of sensation:

> All the myriads of Eternity,
> All the wisdom & joy of life
> Roll like a sea around him,
> Except what his little orbs
> Of sight by degrees unfold. (K 230)

The nightmare of life in the physical world replaces the dynamic and *real* dreams of Eternity: "And now his eternal life/ Like a dream was obliterated."

Los, the representative in us of the Poetic Genius, accepts what we can now call "the world of the senses." The result is the horror at the vast, inhuman universe that is the historical result of the British empirical tradition:

> Los suffer'd his fires to decay;
> Then he look'd back with anxious desire,
> But the space, undivided by existence,
> Struck horror into his soul. (K 230)

Los's error is our error in ratio perception. Even though he is the representative of the imaginative mode of perception, he simply accepts a world "Frozen/ Into horrible forms of deformity" that he himself has created. Instead of demanding change, he feels pity — an emotion that is proof of his imaginative weakness:

> He saw Urizen deadly black
> In his chains bound, & Pity began.
>
> In anguish dividing & dividing,
> For pity divides the soul. . . . (K 230)

The division of the soul of Los produces Enitharmon, the first "female" form; brings the sexes into the world for the first time; and leads toward our kind of existence, which Blake calls "Generation," which has men and women instead of Man. Los has been the creator of space and time, as we have seen; but, from now on, Enitharmon represents space and Los time — indeed, Enitharmon is the first of the many female figures that represent roughly "the natural world" that we will encounter. With the birth of Enitharmon and with the additional disintegration of our imaginative powers that she represents, we are separated even more completely from Eternity; the Imagination (represented in its unfallen power by the Eternals) cannot learn from nature but risks being stifled by it. The Eternals must refuse to contemplate a world with Enitharmon in it:

> "Spread a Tent with strong curtains around them.
> Let cords & stakes bind in the Void,
> That Eternals may no more behold them."
> They began to weave curtains of darkness,
> They erected large pillars round the Void,
> With golden hooks fasten'd in the pillars;
> With infinite labour the Eternals
> A woof wove, and called it Science. (K 231)

What we call "Science," a knowledge based on delusive "nature," is not the truth about our existence but that which separates us from the truth. The Newtonian world machine, a "scientific" model of nature that denies Imagination a role in perception, has been completed.

Yet, even in our world of Space and Time, the fallen Imagination is often open to Eternity. We still have emotions, and some of us are artists. Thus, even within the natural processes of Generation, which otherwise bind us to the earth, a revolutionary possibility can arise. In Chapter VI, which recounts the conception, the life in the womb, and the birth of Orc, we find Blake's usual revolutionary figure and representative of the passionate aspects of our makeup. Orc passes through Generation itself, and his doing so recapitulates what we think is the scientific history of man's origin:

> Coil'd within Enitharmon's womb
> The serpent grew, casting its scales;
> With sharp pangs the hissings began
> To change to a grating cry:
> Many sorrows and dismal throes,
> Many forms of fish, bird & beast
> Brought forth an Infant form
> Where was a worm before. (K 232)

Like the serpent in the Garden, Orc threatens change; and, ironically enough, Los and Enitharmon, who hardly need fear the loss of Paradise *now*, fear the change their offspring represents. Eternity passes seemingly beyond reach as Los accepts the generative cycles. "No more Los beheld Eternity"; instead, he accepts the restrictive patterns of natural life:

> A tight'ning girdle grew
> Around his bosom. In sobbings
> He burst the girdle in twain;
> But still another girdle
> Oppress'd his bosom. In sobbings
> Again he burst it. Again
> Another girdle succeeds.
> The girdle was form'd by day,
> By night was burst in twain. (K 233)

Even though the cycle means "sorrow & pain," Los and Enitharmon so fear change that they insist that Orc be as enchained as they are. To enslave him in this way is to force him to worship Urizen whose "jealous" demand for a world that suits *his* nature created their and our physical world:

> They chain'd his young limbs to the rock
> With the Chain of Jealousy
> Beneath Urizen's deathful shadow. (K 233)

But Orc represents the possibility of revolutionary change. If Los and Enitharmon do not chain him down, if we do not restrain the passionate element in us, revolution will begin that will lead through political change to, finally, a return to Eternity:

> The dead heard the voice of the child
> And began to awake from sleep;
> All things heard the voice of the child
> And began to awake to life. (K 233)

The dead are what we call the living, and Orc invites them back to Eternity, the only real life. But Orc is restrained again and again — historically, seven times, Blake suggests elsewhere — before the movement back to Eternity can begin.

Urizen's "Science" continues to take shape in the remainder of Chapter VII and in Chapter VIII. He invents measuring instruments and tries to understand the physical world about him. He invents the scientific modes of understanding such a world; and he even develops the system of the elements when he causes Thiriel (air), Utha (water), Grodna (earth), and Fuzon (fire) to come into existence. But mankind does not respond so well to Urizen's categories as does the inert physical world that he jealously needs: "he curs'd/ Both sons & daughters; for he saw/ That no flesh nor spirit could keep/ His iron laws one moment." He recognizes that his creation is somehow imperfect ("For he saw that life liv'd upon death:/ The Ox in the slaughter house moans,/ The Dog at the wintry door. . . ."); but his response is entirely the wrong one, for "he wept & he called it Pity. . . ." From this pity for mankind's failure to satisfy his love of rigidity is invented the theology that would explain such human failure to measure up:

> . . . a Web, dark & cold, throughout all
> The tormented element stretch'd
> From the sorrows of Urizen's soul.
> And the Web is a Female in embrio.
> None could break the Web, no wings of fire,
>
> So twisted the cords, & so knotted
> The meshes, twisted like to the human brain.
>
> And all call'd it The Net of Religion. (K 235)

The web is a "female in embrio" because she is that representative of false religion, the Whore of Babylon, who is called Rahab in Blake's system. But the origin of this web is, of course, the human brain.

   With further restrictions, moral and theological, as well as perceptual, in effect for mankind, the human form shrinks even more, as the beginning of Chapter IX explains. Men create themselves as they place limits on their imagination and passions:

> . . . in reptile forms shrinking together,
> Of seven feet stature they remain'd.
>
> Six days they shrunk up from existence,
> And on the seventh day they rested,

> And they blessed the seventh day in sick hope,
> And forgot their eternal life. (K 236)

They bind themselves to the earth, just as Orc was bound:

> No more could they rise at will
> In the infinite void, but bound down
> To earth by their narrowing perceptions
> They lived a period of years;
> Then left a noisom body
> To the jaws of devouring darkness. (K 236)

They accept death, and they accept Urizen's rigid energy-denying laws:

> And their children wept, & built
> Tombs in the desolate places,
> And form'd laws of prudence, and call'd them
> The eternal laws of God. (K 236)

Only Fuzon, the destructive element of fire, and therefore similar to the passionate Orc as an aspect of our makeup, remains to suggest the possibility of change. He does not accept this "Egypt," this land of death and captivity, that we accept. But, for now, like Orc, he simply remains the unrealized potentiality of our ultimate return to the joys of Eternity.

V   *The Blakean Myth*

With the completion of our survey of *The Book of Urizen*, the outlines of Blake's myth are clear. Urizen, Los, Orc, Enitharmon, even Fuzon (and Grodna, Thiriel, and Utha) represent aspects of our own mental life, particularly as it relates to our modes of perception. As literary characters these figures have, of course, no "realistic" appeal at all: they are drawn in the sharp outline form that for Blake constitutes great art, and all accidents of shade are burned away. Nevertheless, Urizen is seen again and again as the white-haired, weeping law giver that we see in the illustrations and text of *The Book of Urizen*. Similarly, Orc remains the dangerous revolutionary boy; and Los continues to represent the spirit of poetry and prophecy that is forced by Urizen to freeze our imaginative world into the delusive forms of ratio perception but that is still capable of hearing the voices of Eternity and of forging that world anew. Los is, despite his fall, nonetheless the imaginative side of us. Fuzon will merge with the figure of Orc, whom he resembles even here, in much of Blake's later work.

Indeed, the exact history of these mythic figures shifts and is retold with additions and changes, throughout Blake's career. Blake's interest is in what they say about our mental condition and history and is not in any "life" of their own that these figures might possess. For Milton, the exact history of Satan's revolt and Adam's fall was worth establishing; but Blake, who knows what our exact mental history is, feels no need to adhere to a frozen set of imaginative equivalents for it.

But the admission of change in Blake's mythic system does not deny that there are important basic outlines within it. Most of the system is revealed in *The Book of Urizen;* but, as Blake subsequently employs it, it is useful to know that the healthy human personality that we all possessed before Urizen's creation of a fixed world comes to be named Albion in Blake's myth. Blake also accepts Albion as a traditional name for England, so that a restored Albion will also represent a reborn England. Albion's emanation — the imaginative world that he and we would inhabit were we not asleep (Albion is often pictured as sleeping, blind to the Eternity about him) — is named Jerusalem. Thus Urizen (roughly, reason), Los (imagination), and Orc (passion) come to represent aspects of Albion's makeup as they represent aspects of our makeup. In Etermity, we learn as we read on in Blake, these figures had different names than they have in Generation. Urizen is an eternal name, but we have so far encountered Los and Orc only after the fall and need to learn their eternal names. Furthermore, there is a fourth aspect of Albion and our personality that we encounter only in later tellings of the myth: his eternal name is Tharmas, and he is representative of the healthy unity of perception that we once possessed.

A chart of some sort is perhaps useful as we begin to read Blake:

	Albion		
eternal name	Urthona	Urizen Tharmas	Luvah
fallen name	Los	Satan	Orc

Los is the earth-owner (Urthona) in Eternity because he, and not Urizen, is the true creator of such imaginative shapes as our fallen perception has frozen into the features of the fallen world. Orc is Luvah ("Lover") in Eternity because there passion has its right name too. Urizen in his fall, which is to say his creation of the world, is Satan, whom we all know to be Prince of this world. The four figures — Los, Orc, Urizen, Tharmas — are called the "four zoas" by Blake because they remind us of the four figures — eagle, lion, ox, and man — around the throne of the Lamb in the Book of Revelations.[8]

The Four Zoas (written 1797–1807) is the most complete working out of the mythic system suggested by *The Book of Urizen;* but Blake wrote *The Book of Ahania* (1795), *The Book of Los* (1795), and *The Song of Los* (1795) as first attempts at a continuation of *The Book of Urizen*'s story of the disintegration of the human mind. In 1794, the year of *The Book of Urizen* itself, Blake also published *Europe* in which he depicts the dominance that an externalized "nature" and a "natural religion" based on "nature" assert over mankind. These shorter works have the same themes as the epics Blake later wrote, and they confirm what *Urizen* has taught us about his mythology and method.

There will be some other details to absorb in our study of Blake's mythological system, but we need little more than what has already been outlined to begin to read Blake's poetry, lyric or epic, with some understanding. When we make the effort to hold the outlines of this myth in mind, we are ready to accept the gift that Blake holds for us:

> I give you the end of a golden string,
>   Only wind it into a ball,
> It will lead you in at Heaven's gate
>   Built in Jerusalem's wall. (*Jerusalem*, K 716)

We can now begin our movement toward a restored perception, toward psychological health, and toward the human Eternity where we can, in Blake's exact definition of man's need, "be happy."

CHAPTER 3

Poetical Sketches

Poetical Sketches (1783) collects poems written by Blake in "untutored youth, commenced in his twelfth, and occasionally resumed by the author till his twentieth year" (K 883). Despite the attempts of some scholars to find a significant correspondence between Blake's fully realized "system," as it appears in the major works of the years to come, and these juvenile experiments in writing verse, it is more accurate to acknowledge, with Stanley Gardner, "how conventional some of the *Poetical Sketches* are." As Gardner recognizes, "Blake wrote later with such uncompromising originality that the ordinariness of the beginning is often forgotten."[1] What any reader of poetry does find, however, are such fine individual lyrics as the unrhymed sonnet "To the Evening Star":

> Thou fair-hair'd angel of the evening,
> Now, while the sun rests on the mountains, light
> Thy bright torch of love; thy radiant crown
> Put on, and smile upon our evening bed!
> Smile on our loves, and, while thou drawest the
> Blue curtains of the sky, scatter thy silver dew
> On every flower that shuts its sweet eyes
> In timely sleep. Let thy west wind sleep on
> The lake; speak silence with thy glimmering eyes,
> And wash the dusk with silver. Soon, full soon,
> Dost thou withdraw; then the wolf rages wide,
> And the lion glares thro' the dun forest:
> The fleeces of our flocks are cover'd with
> Thy sacred dew: protect them with thine influence. (K 3)

And, in the longing for a world protected from the fierce wolves and lions that make up physical life, the student of Blake cannot miss the same longing for Eden that is authenticated in the *Songs of Innocence* and that is later given its place in the "system" as an aspect of human need that only Eternity can satisfy. In fact, if we continue to approach *Poetical Sketches* with the intent of seeking a cast of mind that would only subsequently find adequate expression, we can read the poems of Blake's adolescence with some profit and with undiminished pleasure because of what is done well.

The works are imitative, particularly in subject matter, and are often laced with stock eighteenth-century poetic diction. Yet the longing for a transformed world that is fundamental to Blake's as yet unembodied vision is in "Song" ("Fresh from the dewy hill" [K 9]):

> So when she speaks, the voice of Heaven I hear:
> So when we walk, nothing impure comes near;
> Each field seems Eden, and each calm retreat;
> Each village seems the haunt of holy feet.

Similarly, there seems to be, even in Blake's quite conventional addresses to the four seasons, hints of a habit of mind that links a man's psychology with the type of physical and seasonal environment that he finds himself to be inhabiting. In "To Summer" (K 2), we must possess inspiration and energy to earn summer:

> Our bards are fam'd who strike the silver wire:
> Our youths are bolder than the southern swains:
> Our maidens fairer in the sprightly dance:
> We lack not songs, nor instruments of joy. . . .

The fulfillment that autumn can represent comes in "To Autumn" (K 2) only when man is artist enough to earn it: "O autumn . . . / . . . tune thy jolly voice to my fresh pipe;/ And all the daughters of the year shall dance!" In "To Spring" (K 1), the earth that we inhabit must deserve spring: ". . . put/ Thy golden crown upon her languish'd head,/ Whose modest tresses were bound up for thee!" In "To Winter," that season seems to arrive despite our endeavors; it denies our impulse to participate; but even winter seems to respond to a changed psychological environment: ". . . heaven smiles, and the monster/ Is driv'n yelling to his caves beneath mount Hecla" (K 3).

As Blake's critics have observed, the abstractions in these poems about the seasons are the ancestors of Blake's mythic figures: Winter, with his life-denying assertion of sovereignty, seems particularly to anticipate Urizen. But most important to the student of Blake is simply the recognition that his instinctive assumption in

these poems is that the quality of our participation as perceiver is
related somehow to the quality of the combined mental and physical
environment that we possess.

If we receive the sort of physical environment that we deserve, we
certainly make our own artistic environment. Thus the muses absent
themselves from England in "To the Muses" *because* "The languid
strings do scarcely move!/ The sound is forc'd, the notes are few!"
(K 11). But the most striking poem in the collection, the one that
seems most of all like the work of the adult Blake, is "Mad Song." In
it, we find a man in the mental state that the empirical habits of the
eighteenth century would necessarily encourage. His error is the
solipsism of a Urizen — or a Newton; he "infold[s]" his "griefs" and
sees a closed, inhuman world:

> Lo! to the vault
>   Of paved heaven
> With sorrow fraught
>   My notes are driven. . . . (K 9)

Heaven is "paved" only to the man who chooses to inhabit the world
of ratio vision. Such a man refuses the truth of inspiration and
prefers the darkness that Blake would one day call Ulro:

> After night I do croud,
>   And with night will go;
> I turn my back to the east,
> From whence comforts have increas'd;
> For light doth seize my brain
> With frantic pain. (K 9)

As Blake later recognized, what this world considers as madness in a
poet like Cowper or in Blake himself is "a refuge from unbelief"
(K 772), a refuge from the real madmen, "Bacon, Newton and
Locke," or from anyone who might be the speaker of "Mad Song."

In the instinctive aversion to enclosure within a world whose sky
is, in "Mad Song," "the vault/ Of paved heaven," we also find an
early example of the images of restriction that characterize Blake's
portrayal of our rigid world of physical, political, and moral limitation. Another example is found in "How sweet I roam'd from field to
field" in which Cupid ("the prince of love") captures the speaker in
the tender trap of physical passion:

> He caught me in his silken net,
> And shut me in his golden cage.
>
> He loves to sit and hear me sing,
>   Then, laughing, sports and plays with me;
> Then stretches out my golden wing,
>   And mocks my loss of liberty. (K 6)

Later Blake warns us against the natural heart that ties us to this fallen world of our bad perception. Already we find the beginning of Blake's awareness that "the [visionary] Eye sees more than the Heart knows" and that Imagination must ultimately break the cage into which the natural heart leads us. Indeed, the prose "Contemplation" printed in *Poetical Sketches* has the thoroughly Blakean "I am wrapped in mortality, my flesh is a prison, my bones are bars of death" (K 7). The thought is a usual Christian one, frequently voiced in Blake's time; for the future Bishop of London, Beilby Porteus, had ended his *Death: A Poetical Essay* (1773) with

> . . . my rapt Soul anticipating Heav'n
> Bursts from the thraldom of incumbring clay,
> And on the wing of Extasy upborn
> Springs into Liberty, and Light, and Life.[2]

But, conventional or not, a view of our present life as in every sense a prison seems to have been taking shape in Blake's mind from his earliest days since we are told that "How sweet I roamed" was written when he was fourteen.

Other hints of Blake's future attitudes and interests are found in "Gwin, King of Norway" in the hatred of tyranny it reveals and in the apocalyptic imagery that revolution calls forth:

> The god of war is drunk with blood;
>   The earth doth faint and fail;
> The stench of blood makes sick the heav'ns;
>   Ghosts glut the throat of hell!
>
> O what have Kings to answer for,
>   Before that awful throne!
> When thousand deaths for vengeance cry,
>   And ghosts accusing groan!

> Like blazing comets in the sky,
> That shake the stars of light,
> Which drop like fruit unto the earth
> Thro' the fierce burning night;
>
> Like these did Gwin and Gordred meet. . . . (K 13–14)

Furthermore, we are struck by the appearance of Albion as the future home of Liberty in Blake's pseudo-Shakespearean play "King Edward the Third" because we know that, for the mature Blake, "Jerusalem is named Liberty among the Sons of Albion" and that the return of Jerusalem to Albion will be the theme of Blake's last great epic. Perhaps we can even see the mythic giant Albion himself, though still the traditional "she" that men use when speaking of nations, in the fragment called "Prologue to King John": "O yet may Albion smile again, and stretch her peaceful arms, and raise her golden head, exultingly" (K 34). And when we read in the same brief paragraph that "Tyranny hath stain'd fair Albion's breast with her own children's gore," we think at once of Blake's later assertion that child-sacrifice is the inevitable result and a clear sign of the presence of natural religion. But, in such a search for what is Blakean among these pieces of juvenilia, we find ourselves looking farther and farther into the future to seek points of comparison.

Blake himself seems to have been unwilling to dwell in the past represented by these early productions, for the Reverend A. S. Mathew's apologetic preface tells us that Blake's "talents having been wholly directed to the attainment of excellence in his profession, he has been deprived of the leisure requisite to such a revisal of these sheets, as might have rendered them less unfit to meet the public eye" (K 883). Many readers take Mathew's remark to mean that Blake did not bother to correct the proofs of his poems. Apparently he made no effort to publish the unbound pages that came from his anonymous printers. Perhaps we are wisest to take the hint and to concentrate upon his adult productions.

CHAPTER 4

The Marriage of Heaven and Hell

I *The Theological and Political Context*

EVEN though *The Marriage of Heaven and Hell* (c. 1793) is of particular value to anyone beginning the study of William Blake, it is perhaps unfortunate that this work has come to serve as almost the only one of Blake's, other than a few of his lyrics, that some students ever see. The work is hardly a characteristic production for, largely in prose, it only contains a little poetry; and it is not mythic except in the appended "Song of Liberty" portion. Blake relies in this work on the aphorism and on prose accounts of visionary experiences called "memorable fancies" that are written out of his desire to parody Emanuel Swedenborg's practice in offering "memorable relations" of his visions of Eternity. And even the attitude toward Swedenborg, whether directly presented or implied in the parodies, can mislead us if we view it as Blake's consistent estimate of Swedenborg's value. Although Blake came to resent Swedenborg's apparent belief in predestination and in a conventional system of moral law, he could still recommend the "works of this visionary" as being "well worthy the attention of Painters and Poets" because they are "foundations for grand things" (K 581).[1]

Blake's thought, his language, and his work in the visual arts were indebted throughout his career to Swedenborg. There is a good deal in the resolutions of the Swedenborgian convention of 1789 that Blake could have subscribed to all his life even as he did then. The mature Blake would have agreed with the young Blake "that all Faith and Worship directed to any other, than to the one God Jesus Christ in his Divine Humanity" is "directed to a God invisible and incomprehensible" (the God that Blake calls "Nobodaddy" in one of his Manuscript Notebook poems). Similarly, Blake would always hold that "immediately on the Death of the material body . . . man rises again to his spiritual or substantial body, wherein he existeth in perfect human form."[2] Blake's habit of speaking of the Divine Humanity and of using the human form as the index of perfection is the most striking of the results of his exposure to Swedenborg's thought.

Blake's quarrel with Swedenborg in *The Marriage* is, therefore, limited to subsidiary points.[3] Indeed, Blake seems to evince some resentment of Swedenborg's presumption to exclusive possession of visionary powers that see truths not available to the conventionally religious (whom Blake calls the "religious"): Swedenborg "imagines that all are religious, & himself the single one on earth that ever broke a net" (K 157). The reason for Swedenborg's presumption, Blake feels, is his lack of contact with other energetic and visionary men like Paracelsus and Jacob Boehme, or like Dante and Shakespeare: Swedenborg "conversed with Angels who are all religious, & conversed not with Devils who all hate religion . . ." (K 157).

Not only have visionary men broken nets before, but to Blake in 1790 it seems that all of Western civilization is breaking nets. The French Revolution is under way, and the revolutionary spark will spread from France to bring political change, of course, but also to restore our fallen perception: "Now is the dominion of Edom [France], & the return of Adam into Paradise . . ." (K 149). Blake is delighted, at this moment in time, to find himself thirty-three years old, the age of Christ at the Resurrection. He has himself undergone something of a resurrection, having refused Swedenborg his total allegiance ("Swedenborg is the Angel sitting at the tomb: his writings are the linen clothes folded up" [K 149].); but he still relishes Swedenborg's having identified the year of Blake's birth as the beginning of the return to Paradise (". . . a new heaven is begun, and it is now thirty-three years since its advent . . ." [K 149].) Too long the conventionally religious person ("the sneaking serpent" who "walks in mild humility") has tyrannized over the mental life of man while "the just man rages in the wilds." Now, in 1790, Blake feels that the rebirth of mankind in France and the resurrection of the spirit that he has undergone are proof of the freeing of the energy (meaning both passion and imagination) that will restore the just man to his place — no matter what fears such a restoration might strike in the hearts of the pious ("the Eternal Hell revives").

II *Blake's Quarrel with Rational Theology and Morality*

Like Urizen, and unlike Blake, the typical Christian of the eighteenth century has stressed rules for conduct so strongly that he has falsified his own nature. In denying everything that is energetic in himself and in saying that "Good is the passive that obeys Reason . . ./ Evil is the active springing from Energy," he has accepted the theology of a John Milton, who, Blake says, pictures God as "Destiny," Jesus as "a Ratio of the five senses," and the Holy Ghost as "Vacuum." Such Christians are in religion what Sir Joshua Reynolds is in art — the enemies of Inspiration. As the Evangelical clergyman Joseph Milner put it, "Reason . . . has impertinently meddled with the Gospel, and that with such overwhelming sedulity as to darken it more and more. . . ."[4] Blake must offer some fundamental truths to such Christians:

1. Man has no Body distinct from his Soul; for that call'd Body is a portion of Soul discern'd by the five Senses, the chief inlets of Soul in this age.
2. Energy is the only life, and is from the Body; and Reason is the bound or outward circumference of Energy.
3. Energy is Eternal Delight. (K 149)

The conventionally religious follow Urizen in his rage for oneness, but the truth is that we are made up of forces in perpetual conflict: reason is good, but only in its function of setting limits for energy. These opposing forces in mankind, both sides of which must be recognized, are called "contraries" by Blake: "Without Contraries is no progression. Attraction and Repulsion, Reason and Energy, Love and Hate, are necessary to Human existence" (K 149). In Eternity, life is dynamic because it is characterized by that opposition of contraries which is "intellectual War"; but Urizen and most Christians choose our fixed world of fallen perception and of rigid moral categories.

Blake's purpose in *The Marriage of Heaven and Hell* is, then, a restoration of energy's rightful place in a world dominated by reason. With such a restoration there will come about, most importantly, a better understanding of the Jesus who is the human Imagination. For Blake, Jesus is not the rational law giver of many eighteenth-century Christians; he is "all virtue, and acted from impulse, not rules." In this re-evaluation of Jesus, Blake anticipates the direction of much later theology in which "The 'eschatological' or 'apocalyptic' Jesus emerges . . . hardly the teacher of secular morality."[5] As Blake wittily puts the same point, "If Morality was Christianity, Socrates was the Saviour" (K 775).

To restore energy, as well as an energetic Jesus, to its rightful place, Blake employs shock tactics based on a reversal of values that make him the devil's spokesman. For such a reversal he perversely cites the example of John Milton who perhaps wrote his greatest poetry in the speeches of Satan: "Note: The reason Milton wrote in fetters when he wrote of Angels & God, and at liberty when of Devils & Hell, is because he was a true Poet and of the Devil's party without knowing it" (K 150). The vehicle for Blake's "Infernal wisdom" is the Memorable Fancy, a parody of Swedenborg's "Memorable Relations." In the five Memorable Fancies of *The Marriage of Heaven and Hell*, Blake interviews conventional angels and energetic devils. The hells that he visits seem to be places filled with terror to the conventional mind; but Blake walks "among the fires of hell, delighted with the enjoyments of Genius, which to Angels look like torment and insanity."

In the first Memorable Fancy, Blake finds a devil who with "corroding fires," in imitation of Blake's methods as an engraver, has inscribed a cliff-face with this crucial sentence: "How do you know but ev'ry Bird that cuts the airy way, Is an immense world of delight, clos'd by your senses five?" (K 150). With this reminder, we place all that Blake has so far said in *The Marriage of Heaven and Hell* within the context of Blake's views on perception. Our perception *closes* the objects of the world and thereby denies their energy in our desire for Urizenic fixity, a process that renders a human world inhuman. As we move back toward Eternity, the frozen world opens again, and the particles that make up the physical world (the Spectres of the Dead) come to life to reveal themselves as "human," as products of the Divine Imagination in each of us. We can start the return to Eternity ourselves by giving energy its proper role.

Blake announces that he has collected "Proverbs of Hell" that "show the nature of Infernal wisdom." In the Proverbs, we are called to a recognition of the value of impulse:

Prudence is a rich, ugly old maid courted by Incapacity.
He who desires but acts not, breeds pestilence.

. . . .

The apple tree never asks the beech how he shall grow;
nor the lion, the horse, how he shall take his prey.

. . . .

Sooner murder an infant in its cradle than nurse unacted desires. (K 151–52)

Moreover, the inadequacy of our present modes of perception is stressed: "The roaring of lions, the howling of wolves, the raging of the stormy sea, and the destructive sword, are portions of eternity, too great for the eye of man" (K 151).

The superior truth of Vision is asserted:

A fool sees not the same tree that a wise man sees.

. . . .

What is now proved was once only imagin'd.

. . . .

Every thing possible to be believ'd is an image of truth.

. . . .

Where man is not, nature is barren. (K 151–52)

The value of imaginative creativity as the way out of time and back into Eternity is celebrated: "Eternity is in love with the productions of time" (K 151). And, because it is true for Blake that the existence of institutionalized moral prohibition creates the vice it condemns, "Prisons are built with stones of Law, Brothels with bricks of Religion" (K 151). Indeed, the "Proverbs of Hell" in their cryptic way contain most of Blake's doctrine in capsule form: restrictive moral laws and oppressive institutions keep us from the truth and the joy that are in Imagination and energy.

III   *Cleansing the Gates of Perception*

The second Memorable Fancy concerns the subject of perception and contains a good explanation of what Blake means by seeing *through* the eye rather than *with* it. In this section, he converses with the prophets Isaiah and Ezekiel and receives an explanation from Isaiah of what he meant by saying "God spoke" to him: "I saw no God, nor heard any, in a finite organical perception." The conversation continues:

Then I asked: "does a firm perswasion that a thing is so, make it so?"

He replied: "All poets believe that it does, & in ages of imagination this firm perswasion removed mountains; but many are not capable of a firm perswasion of any thing." (K 153)

As Blake said in his annotations to his copy of Berkeley's *Siris:* "Knowledge is not by deduction, but Immediate by Perception or Sense at once. Christ addresses himself to the man, not to his Reason" (K 774). Thus "firm perswasion" is both the voice of God and the authentic vision that sees through the eye. The great contribution of the prophets of Israel was to teach that "the Poetic Genius . . . was the first principle."

We can possess the visionary powers of Isaiah and Ezekiel if we choose. When we return to vision, "the whole creation will be consumed and appear infinite and holy, whereas it now appears finite & corrupt." For us, because our Urizenic tendency is to restrain the Imagination and to repress energy, "This [restoration of infinity] will come to pass by an improvement of sensual enjoyment." Sex is the single imaginative act that most men find possible. If we remove the notion "that man has a body distinct from his soul," sex itself becomes proof of the powers of the Imagination that can tear down the frozen physical world that seems to surround us. Blake awaits our return to vision:

If the doors of perception were cleansed every thing would appear to man as it is, infinite.

For man has closed himself up, till he sees all things thro' narrow chinks of his cavern. (K 154)

But, as the third Memorable Fancy shows, the inside of the cavern can be made infinite by means of Imagination and art.

The fourth Memorable Fancy is a visit to the hell of the conventionally religious — a hell appropriately reached by means of Blake's usual symbol of self-enclosure, the mill. This hell is, like the fallen world that we inhabit, full of threatening objects that we cannot manage without vision: a leviathan striped like a tiger intimidates us "owing to our metaphysics" (as does Blake's famous Tyger), but it does not frighten Blake. Instead, he shows the conventionally religious the hell that they already inhabit in their life in this world:

. . . soon we saw seven houses of brick; one we enter'd; in it were a number of monkeys, baboons, & all of that species, chain'd by the middle, grinning and snatching at one another, but withheld by the shortness of their chains: however, I saw that they sometimes grew numerous, and then the weak were caught by the strong, and with a grinning aspect, first coupled with, & then devour'd, by plucking off first one limb and then another, till the body was left a helpless trunk; this, after grinning & kissing it with seeming fondness, they devour'd too; and here & there I saw one savourily picking the flesh off of his own tail; as the stench terribly annoy'd us both, we went into the mill, & I in my hand brought the skeleton of a body, which in the mill was Aristotle's Analytics. (K 157)

The subhuman nature of the inhabitants and their cannibalism remind us what the solipsistic, rational, and analytic mind does to us at every moment of our lives.

IV *Breaking the Restraining Nets*

The final Memorable Fancy is Blake's defense of the Jesus of impulse. In words that D. H. Lawrence would echo, Blake calls for a recognition of God's presence in the individual man: "The worship of God is: Honouring his gifts in other men, each according to his genius, and loving the greatest men best: those who envy or calumniate great men hate God; for there is no other God" (K 158). Although Lawrence would not agree, Blake holds that the mode of God's participation in us is Jesus, the human Imagination. As Blake says in his annotations to Berkeley, "man is all Imagination. God is Man & exists in us & we in him (K 775).

Jesus would hardly have come, therefore, to accuse us of sin; He came to unite us to Him by restoring us to the Imagination. Again the annotations to Berkeley may be cited: "The Whole Bible is fill'd with Imagination & Visions from End to End & not with Moral Virtues; that is the business of Plato & the Greeks & all Warriors. The Moral virtues are continual Accusers of Sin & promote Eternal Wars & Dominency over others" (K 774). "Jesus is the greatest man," He therefore "acted from impulse, not from rules." Systems of moral virtue produce warfare and political tyranny: "One Law for the Lion & Ox is Oppression." We must recognize the energetic Jesus within our own impulses and allow Him to restore us to what we potentially are.

To make sure that the special significance of the outbreak of the French Revolution, as a representation of the growth in vision to which Blake would lead us, is not lost, he appends a "Song of Liberty" to *The Marriage of Heaven and Hell*. Nature itself is shaken by the freeing acts in France ("the Eternal Female groan'd"). Political change is seen as now possible in England ("Albion"), in America, in Spain, and in Rome. The revolutionary energies of Orc ("the new born fire") are released, and Urizen's ("the starry king") attempts to subdue him to "the hand of jealousy" seem ineffective. The hope held out by Blake is for an end not only to political oppression but to an alienation from our potential greatness that we have suffered: "Look up! look up! O citizen of London, enlarge thy countenance! O Jew, leave counting gold! return to thy oil and wine. O African! black African! (go, winged thought, widen his forehead)" (K 159).

The body, which is not distinct from the soul, finds more human proportions despite Urizen's attempts at resistance. Urizen cannot stop man's development by opposing it with his system of moral virtues because the energetic Orc "stamps the stony law to dust." No longer, says the chorus, are we to "lay the bound or build the roof" of conventional morality: "For every thing that lives is Holy" (K 160). To Blake, the accusation of sin is Satan's function. Life is from the Imagination, which is divine; nothing imaginative can be sinful, despite the protests of "the Priests of the Raven of dawn."

The Marriage of Heaven and Hell in its recommendation of energy, imagination, and impulse is a fine sourcebook for Blake's thought. We can turn to it for Blake's clear and witty warnings against the denial of energy and for his assertion that firm persuasion is truth, and we can also find in it Blake's clear statement of Milton's limitations and Swedenborg's. It is perhaps not so major a creation for Blake the poet, however, as are his mythic works; for its insight into the mind is not earned through our participation in mental processes transformed into events like those in *The Book of Urizen*. As a critique of Swedenborg's limitations, the form and the content of *The Marriage* bear too many signs of an occasional work that depends on a parody of the opponent's methods to make debater's points. But this work was at least the necessary refusal on Blake's part to be enslaved by another man's system, even when that man is another great visionary. Its own energy is at any rate full proof of the presence in Blake of the aspect of our humanity that the work would restore to us.

CHAPTER 5

The French Revolution *and* America

BLAKE'S *The French Revolution*, which exists only in a publisher's proof sheet dated 1791, is prefaced with an Advertise-
ment that announces that "The remaining Books of this Poem are
finished, and will be published in their Order." We have only "Book
the First," but it is quite possible that *The French Revolution* was
indeed finished by Blake as a poem in seven books. Joseph Johnson,
who would have been the publisher, apparently lost his nerve when
it came to the actual publication of a poem so strongly in favor of the
revolution in France — as he had done in the case of Thomas Paine's
book *The Rights of Man* — but Johnson was an unusually
scrupulous publisher who would not be likely to misrepresent the
work he meant to offer to the public.

I *History Made Myth*

The French Revolution, like the later work *America* (1793), is
remarkable among Blake's poems for presenting a landscape
halfway between history and myth. Events of the revolutionary
period in France are presented in a recognizable form, but their
significance is revealed through apocalyptic imagery and through
the actual appearance in the poem, in a dream, of Urizen. Many
other poems by Blake have historical meanings, perhaps all do;[1] but
the historical events are usually fully translated into mythic ones as
in, for instance, "The Mental Traveller," in which political revolution and reaction are seen in terms of contentions between a
tormented Orc figure and an old woman who represents nature. In
The French Revolution, we seem to see the very *process* by which
the visionary eye sees through history to the reality beyond it.

The work as we have it is a presentation of the fears of the nobility
on the eve of the revolution in France. Lafayette (called "Fayette"
by Blake), a leader of the Commons, awaits the charge to lead the

army from Paris. The nobles feel, correctly, that the removal of the army will allow a popular uprising. Most of the poem deals with the responses in debate of the nobility to the mood of pre-revolutionary France — although not all of them fear the "fire" of revolt. At the end of the work as it exists, the Commons recommends that La-fayette proceed to remove the troops; and the fears of the nobility seem confirmed, at least in Blake's visionary treatment of the event.

The debate of the nobility is often reminiscent of the one that had ensued in England after the Reverend Richard Price had preached his sermon welcoming the French Revolution. There followed not only the famous reply by Burke in favor of the old order but also numerous replies to Burke that included such notable works as Paine's *Rights of Man* and Godwin's *Political Justice*. Those who favored the Revolution, especially in the Unitarian circles that in-cluded Dr. Price, Joseph Priestley, and Blake's almost-publisher Joseph Johnson, often saw it as comprised of events that fitted the pattern of the last things set forth in the Book of Revelations.[2] Blake too sees the events as a prelude to apocalypse; but he regards them, characteristically, as the freeing of restrictions on our behavior and perception that starts our return to Eternity. Indeed, he sees the events so totally in the visionary manner that we realize that specific political events, although there are some here, take a definite second place in Blake's mind. Political events for Blake "occur" only as a manifestation of prior mental events — a manner of looking at revolution that seems well justified in at least so "intellectual" a revolution as that in France.

All revolutions are, in fact, directed against Urizen, the jealous law giver and lover of order. Thus Louis XVI appears at the outset of Blake's *French Revolution* in a state of disorganization; from the perspective of Eternity, he is "Sick," "wreath'd in dim/ And appall-ing mist," "cold." His attempt to keep the "mountains" of a Urizenic perspective fixed is, however, now failing: the mountains, the rocky world of our perception, seek to be the "mild flourishing mountains" of Eternity again rather than "the old mountains of France, like aged men." The old order in France is, of course, the result of the vision of "aged men," of Urizenic lawgiving and nar-rowness. When the King descends to visit his nobles, he joins a den of solipsistic Urizens:

Forty men, each conversing with woes in the infinite shadows of his soul,
Like our ancient fathers in regions of twilight, walk, gathering round the
King. . . . (K 134)

The councillors themselves form an enclosure that keeps the King blind to the morning that the rest of France now sees dawning.

From the King, who is, in fact, "imprisoned" by his nobles, we move to the governor of the Bastille, who also wears mental chains:

. . . in his soul stood the purple plague,
Tugging his iron manacles, and piercing through the seven towers dark and sickly,
Panting over the prisoners like a wolf gorg'd. . . . (K 135)

The prisoners watched over by the governor are the unwilling victims of the perceptual and physical tyranny of the old order. A man with the prophetic and Orc-like "serpent coil'd round in his heart" lives in chains for espousing Liberty. Similarly, in "the Den named Religion," a woman who would advocate the forgiveness of sins and consequently denounce the moral categories of a Urizen ("she refus'd to be whore to the minister") is punished with the Law in the form of the seven deadly sins ("The seven diseases of earth"). And a man who "rais'd a pulpit/ And taught wonders to darken'd souls" has the most complete punishment of all:

In the tower nam'd Order, an old man, whose white beard cover'd the stone floor like weeds
On margin of the sea, shrivel'd up by heat of day and cold of night; his den was short
And narrow as a grave dug for a child. . . . (K 135–36)

He has been turned into a Urizen, the perfected ideal of the old order. Another who "pined/ For liberty" has been given the Newtonian universe on which the natural religionists meditate:

. . . his reason decay'd, and the world of attraction in his bosom
Center'd and the rushing of chaos overwhelm'd his dark soul. . . . (K 136)

The Bastille might indeed be taken to represent the universe, moral and "physical," that Urizen brought into being.

II   *The Debate over "mind-forged manacles"*

After all the images of darkness and restriction that we have found in the description of the Bastille, the imagery based on light and new birth that surrounds the meeting of the Commons is all the more welcome:

. . . a light walks round the dark towers:
For the Commons convene in the Hall of the Nation, like spirits of fire in the beautiful
Porches of the Sun, to plant beauty in the desert craving abyss, they gleam
On the anxious city; all children new-born first behold them; tears are fled,
And they nestle in earth-breathing bosoms. So the city of Paris, their wives and children,
Look up to the morning Senate, and visions of sorrow leave pensive streets.
(K 136)

Among the nobles, however, there are only "jealousies," "terrors," and "gloom." They remain "lock'd up as with strong bands of iron, each strong limb bound down as with marble/ In flames of red wrath burning. . . ." And, as yet, no one instructs them in the uses of fire.

The King again expresses his fears, and the Duke of Burgundy rises to confirm them. Because the Duke will act to check the possibility of new birth, "Around him croud, weeping in his burning robe,/ A bright cloud of infant souls; his words fall like purple autumn on the sheaves":

"Shall this marble-built heaven become a clay cottage, this earth an oak stool, and these mowers
From the Atlantic mountains mow down all this great starry harvest of six thousand years?
And shall Necker, the hind of Geneva, stretch out his crook'd sickle o'er fertile France
Till our purple and crimson is faded to russet, and the kingdoms of earth bound in sheaves,
And the ancient forests of chivalry hewn, and the joys of combat burnt for fuel;
Till the power and dominion is rent from the pole, sword and scepter from sun and moon,
The law and gospel from fire and air, and eternal reason and science
From the deep and the solid, and man lay his faded head down on the rock
Of eternity, where the eternal lion and eagle remain to devour? (K 138)

Rather than the human scale of "a clay cottage" and an "oak stool," Burgundy (like Louis) demands the stony world of Urizen ("marble-built heaven"). To Blake, "forests" are signs of Urizenic delusion, and he would say that there can be "joys of combat" only when wars are entirely mental; but Burgundy joins Edmund Burke in bemoaning the end of an age of chivalry.[3] And, since all error is one in

Blake's thought, Burgundy also defends natural religion — that confused state of mind in which one seeks "The law and gospel" in the elements and thinks that science has something to do with "the deep and the solid" rather than the imaginative.

With a Burgundy to support his worst tendencies, Louis allows "dark mists" to "roll round" him "and blot the writing of God/ Written" within his "bosom." Necker, who would sympathize with the Commons as Burgundy fears, is driven out of the court; and the Archbishop of Paris rises to complete the consolidation of error: ". . . the Archbishop of Paris arose/ In the rushing of scales and hissing of flames and/ rolling of sulphurous smoke" (K 139-40). Not only are his fires entirely perverted into infernal flames, but he is well on his way to becoming a member of that snake pit that is the final state of the forces of evil in Milton's *Paradise Lost.*

Of course, the Archbishop speaks of visions of Urizen:

. . . a cold hand passed over my limbs, and behold
An aged form, white as snow, hov'ring in mist, weeping in the uncertain light.
Dim the form almost faded, tears fell down the shady cheeks. . . . (K 140)

Urizen sees in the coming of the revolution the danger that men will "forget" his "holy law." He fears the end of the alliance of church and state in what is to him a necessary tyranny:

. . . Nobles and Clergy shall fail from before me, and my cloud and vision be no more;
The mitre become black, the crown vanish, and the scepter and ivory staff
Of the ruler wither among bones of death. . . . (K 140)

He fears the end of forms and hierarchies:

They shall drop at the plow and faint at the harrow, unredeem'd, unconfess'd, unpardon'd;
The priest rot in his surplice by the lawless lover, the holy beside the accursed,
The King, frowning in purple, beside the grey plowman, and their worms embrace together. (K 140-41)

Urizen's fears are quite justified; for, to Blake, revolution does mean an end to moral categories and to privilege of all sorts. The effect of Urizen's speech on the nobles is, understandably, to so fix them in reaction that the weeping infants surrounding them are replaced by their own deformed spawn: "monsters of worlds unknown/ Swam round them watching to be delivered." The Archbishop of Paris is himself now totally a snake, Blake's usual image for the evils of priestcraft: he is unable to rise to his feet and "instead of words harsh hissings/ Shook the chamber."

Next, the defenders of the revolution and of Imagination speak. The first, the Duke of Orleans, undertakes the task of trying to bring the nobles to an understanding of their own natures: . . . " 'O princes of fire, whose flames are for growth, not consuming,/ Fear not dreams, fear not visions, nor be you dismay'd with sorrows which flee at the morning!' " (K 142). A man's fire — his energy and his imagination — is not to be feared and repressed: "Fire delights in its form,"; and one man can not make laws to govern another's flames:

". . . Go, thou cold recluse, into the fires
Of another's high flaming rich bosom, and return, unconsum'd, and write laws.
If thou canst not do this, doubt thy theories; learn to consider all men as thy equals,
Thy brethren, and not as thy foot or thy hand, unless thou first fearest to hurt them." (K 142–43)

All men are equal because all possess the Divine Imagination, and any political or theological system that denies this fact is tyrannous.

The Abbé de Sieyès arrives from the Commons to complete the education of the nobles:

"When the heavens were seal'd with a stone, and the terrible sun clos'd in an orb, and the moon
Rent from the nations, and each star appointed for watchers of night,
The millions of spirits immortal were bound in the ruins of sulphur heaven
To wander enslav'd; black, deprest in dark ignorance, kept in awe with the whip
To worship terrors, bred from the blood of revenge and breath of desire
In bestial forms, or more terrible men; till the dawn of our peaceful morning,
Till dawn, till morning, till the breaking of clouds, and swelling of winds, and the universal voice;
Till man raise his darken'd limbs out of the caves of night; his eyes and his heart
Expand: where is Space? where, O Sun, is thy dwelling? where thy tent, O faint slumb'rous Moon?" (K 143–44)

What the nobles fear as political revolution is in fact a movement away from closed perception and from an alienation from their real selves. A world of peace, love, and art is promised:

". . . the saw, and the hammer, the chisel, the pencil, the pen, and the instruments
Of heavenly song sound in the wilds once forbidden, to teach the laborious plowman
And shepherd, deliver'd from clouds of war, from pestilence, from night-fear, from murder,
From falling, from stifling, from hunger, from cold, from slander, discontent and sloth,
That walk in beasts and birds of night, driven back by the sandy desart
Like pestilent fogs round cities of men; and the happy earth sing in its course,
The mild peaceable nations be opened to heav'n, and men walk with their fathers in bliss." (K 144–45)

But the nobles cannot understand these words as anything but a threat.

III   *The Political Road to Apocalypse*

When the Commons orders Lafayette to lead the army away, the visionary meaning of his obedience to their command is made evident by Blake:

Like a flame of fire he stood before dark ranks, and before expecting captains:
On pestilent vapours around him flow frequent spectres of religious men, weeping
In winds, driven out of the abbeys, their naked souls shiver in keen open air;
Driven out by the fiery cloud of Voltaire, and thund'rous rocks of Rousseau,
They dash like foam against the ridges of the army, uttering a faint feeble cry. (K 146)

Voltaire and Rousseau, men whose views Blake fiercely opposed, are nonetheless valuable to the imaginative man because of their opposition to institutionalized religion. The serpent-nobility surround the King, who seems in any case near death ("Pale and cold . . . his pulses/ Suspended"):

    The cold newt
And snake and damp toad on the kingly foot crawl, or croak on the awful knee,

Shedding their slime; in folds of the robe the crown'd adder builds and hisses
From stony brows; shaken the forests of France, sick the kings of the nations,
And the bottoms of the world were open'd, and the graves of archangels unseal'd:
The enormous dead lift up their pale fires and look over the rocky cliffs.
(K 147–48)

The forests of error, the stony world itself, await the apocalypse. Repressed energy and vision ("The enormous dead") are free at last. There is much more of the story to be told, but the debaters of Book I have moved us to the margins of Eternity as Blake's contending forces so often do. For a while, it must have seemed to Blake that real political events could be used to suggest the growth in mental powers that he invites us to participate in; for *The French Revolution*, with its willingness to see both with and through the eye, was the happy result of this feeling.

IV   An American Analogue

Although the revolution in nearby France would continue to influence English civilization and politics for years to come, the revolutionary period in Western history had of course opened with the American Revolution. Having written *The French Revolution*, Blake turned to the earlier American events and interpreted them as similarly apocalyptic signs. *America* (1793) needs less commentary than *The French Revolution* because it is a less difficult work.

An American reader is gratified to find George Washington, Benjamin Franklin, Tom Paine, John Hancock, and other American heroes allied with a fiery adolescent Orc in a rebellion that simultaneously rejects delusive Nature and George III. The imagery is that of the Resurrection ("The grave is burst, the spices shed, the linen wrapped up. . . .") because the events in America are a first step on the way to a reborn Divine Humanity that is free of restrictive moral codes and life-denying institutions:

The doors of marriage are open, and the Priests in rustling scales
Rush into reptile coverts, hiding from the fires of Orc,
That play around the golden roofs in wreaths of fierce desire,
Leaving the females naked and glowing with the lusts of youth.
For the female spirits of the dead, pining in bonds of religion,

Run from their fetters reddening, & in long drawn arches sitting,
They feel the nerves of youth renew, and desires of ancient times
Over their pale limbs, as a vine when the tender grape appears. (K 202)

Thus, in *America,* as in *The French Revolution,* Blake demonstrates that any step taken in behalf of freedom is a step toward the perfect liberty of Eternity. In both works he retains recognizable historical events and persons while supplying their visionary meanings. In these works Blake shows us how he read the events of his time and forces us to speculate about how he would read the events of our own times, if he were to look for signs of success for Imagination and energy.

CHAPTER 6

Visions of the Daughters of Albion

WILLIAM Blake offered his vigorous support to the cause of women's liberation when he wrote *Visions of the Daughters of Albion* (1793). The restrictions placed on women are the result of jealousy, a quality exemplified in Urizen, and jealousy demands an environment where all will submit to control and be subject to "one law." Since the emotion of jealousy always exists in the "natural heart" that we possess in our fallen condition, Blake's epigraph for the *Visions* is "The Eye sees more than the [natural] Heart knows"; for Vision can break through the nets of jealousy.

The heroine of the *Visions of the Daughters of Albion* is Oothoon, who is "the soft soul of America" and who is, therefore, the representative of liberty, as is Jerusalem. Her plight, her unsatisfied aspiration for liberty, is the plight of all the women of England; and this poem is a visionary insight into their condition. But in another sense we are all, male and female, the "daughters of Albion" who await the restoration of our liberty. ("Jerusalem is named liberty/ Among the sons of Albion [K 649].) To keep the universality of Oothoon's plight before us, Blake throughout uses "the daughters of Albion" as something of a chorus: "Enslav'd, the daughters of Albion weep: a trembling lamentation/ Upon their mountains; in their valleys, sighs towards America" (K 189); "The Daughters of Albion hear her woes, & eccho back her sighs" (K 190). The device effectively reminds us that we must seek for a solution to Oothoon's dilemma by exploring our own lives and minds.

The events of the poem are few. Oothoon had hesitated in her "virgin fears" to undertake a physical relationship with Theotormon, whom she loves. But, told by the Marygold that "the soul of sweet delight/ Can never pass away," she learns that the loss of virginity is not — despite the attitudes of her culture — a change in identity. ("Every Harlot was a Virgin once," Blake writes elsewhere. "Nor can'st thou ever change Kate into Nan" [K 771].) But, before she can find Theotormon, presumably simply to marry him, she is attacked by an "accuser of sin" who might be Urizen or Satan but who is named Bromion. Bromion brands her a "harlot" for her attitudes, and Theotormon then fears her too. As a result, Bromion, an accuser of sin, and Oothoon, a representative of liberty, are tied back to back in a cave by the "jealous" Theotormon (whose name probably means "God-tormented," one tortured by holding the mistaken vision of God the lawgiver rather than of the Jesus who preaches "mutual forgiveness of sins").

A debate follows among these three about the issues of freedom and restraint; but no resolution occurs because nothing has yet changed for the daughters of Albion. Nonetheless, the debate tells us much about the origins of some of our most fundamental attitudes. Bromion's labeling of Oothoon as a harlot is a Urizenic assertion of control over her that is the same act of mind that allows one man to own another in the institution of slavery:

> Bromion spoke: "Behold this harlot here on Bromion's bed,
> And let the jealous dolphins sport around the lovely maid!
> Thy soft American plains are mine, and mine thy north & south:
> Stampt with my signet are the swarthy children of the sun;
> They are obedient, they resist not, they obey the scourge;
> Their daughters worship terrors and obey the violent." (K 190)

And the label "harlot" is similarly the challenge to Theotormon's male pride that forces him to perform his jealous act of binding Oothoon to Bromion, her accuser. Thus he too holds attitudes that have perpetuated social evils: ". . . beneath him sound like waves on a desart shore/ The voice of slaves beneath the sun, and children bought with money,/ That shiver in religious caves . . ." (K 190).

Social evil, corrupt institutions, poverty, and war are all the result of our faulty vision for Blake: could our perspective be changed, all "external" to us would change. Oothoon alone can see clearly because she is "the soft soul of America," and she has picked the Marygold. "Arise, my Theotormon," she pleads, "I am pure"; and she offers an account of that fundamental error in perception that has created all our misery:

> "They told me that the night & day were all that I could see;
> They told me that I had five senses to inclose me up,

And they inclos'd my infinite brain into a narrow circle,
And sunk my heart into the Abyss, a red, round globe, hot burning,
Till all from life I was obliterated and erased." (K 191)

She begs us to remember that impulse would have a major role to play if we were to heed it: "ask . . . the wing'd eagle why he loves the sun;/ And then tell me the thoughts of man, that have been hid of old." But no one understands what she is saying.

Theotormon is so Urizenic in his attitudes by now that any appeal based on the value of impulse is meaningless to him (". . . what is the night or day to one o'erflow'd with woe?"). Instead, he wants what jealousy always wants — a rigid, fixed world:

"Tell me what is a thought, & of what *substance* is it made?
Tell me what is a joy, & *in what gardens* do joys grow?
And *in what rivers* swim the sorrows? and *upon what mountains*
Wave shadows of discontent? and *in what houses* dwell the wretched,
Drunken with woe forgotten, and shut up from cold despair?"
(K 191–92; italics added)

Theotormon's demand that thoughts be things ("substance") and have physical location ("in what gardens . . . in what rivers . . . upon what mountains . . . in what houses") exactly repeats the error in perception that creates our physical world. Bromion's condition is even more diseased; for, not contented with *one* physical world to possess in jealous vision, he wants more such worlds. He seeks them even "in the infinite microscope," an activity absurd to Blake, who knows that the observer brings his own fallen vision to what is called "scientific observation" and sees, therefore, only his own limitations in what he thinks he investigates. As happened with Urizen, Bromion's mistaken sense that fixity can exist and is desirable produces not just the sort of physical world he inhabits but the kind of moral world he would try to force on mankind: "And is there not one law for both the lion and the ox?/ And is there not eternal fire and eternal chains/ To bind the phantoms of existence from eternal life?" (K 192). Not sharing Oothoon's new understanding of the possibilities for cleansing the gates of perception, Bromion and Theotormon can never understand her arguments for a new view of morality.

Oothoon rightly attacks Urizen, who in Blake's myth is largely responsible for all that we endure:

"O Urizen! Creator of men! mistaken Demon of heaven!
Thy joys are tears, thy labour vain to form men to thine image.
How can one joy absorb another? are not different joys
Holy, eternal, infinite? And each joy is a Love." (K 192)

She talks about the treatment of women in our civilization
("bound/ In spells of law to one she loathes") and of female and
male masturbation (lines 3–7, plate 7, K 194) as "the places of
religion, the rewards of continence,/ The self enjoyings of self
denial." Abhorring all secrecy, she herself welcomes openness and
sunshine:

"Open to joy and to delight where ever beauty appears;
If in the morning sun I find it, there my eyes are fix'd
In happy copulation; if in evening mild, wearied with work,
Sit on a bank and draw the pleasures of this free born joy."
. . . .
"I cry: Love! Love! Love! happy happy Love! free as the mountain wind!"
. . . .
"Arise, and drink your bliss, for every thing that lives is holy!" (K 194–95)

Theotormon, who understands none of her declaration, turns from
the possibility of sunshine and converses "with shadows dire."
    Oothoon even suggests a kind of shock treatment to let Theotor-
mon see that jealousy is not a necessary part of our makeup:

". . . silken nets and traps of adamant will Oothoon spread,
And catch for thee girls of mild silver, or of furious gold.
I'll lie beside thee on a bank & view their wanton play
In lovely copulation, bliss on bliss, with Theotormon:
Red as the rosy morning, lustful as the first born beam,
Oothoon shall view his dear delight, nor e'er with jealous cloud
Come in the heaven of generous love, nor selfish blightings bring."
(K 194–95)

It is perhaps just as well that Theotormon is not given a chance to
reply to this suggestion. Oothoon's world and perception are
perhaps shockingly open, but Theotormon's are tragically closed.
And, while such "jealousy" exists, the women of England cannot be
free — and all men will inhabit this world of "substance" and "one
law."

CHAPTER 7

Songs of Innocence and of Experience

BLAKE had published the *Songs of Innocence* (1789) and the *Songs of Experience* (c.1793) before their appearance together in 1794; but only when he linked those works with the new title *Songs of Innocence and of Experience* (1794) did he complete the execution of the complex and masterful work that contains his most widely read poetry. Much of the greatness of the work for any reader, and at any level that he might read it, arises from the juxtaposition of two modes of vision — Innocence and Experience. Blake's subtitle tells us that these modes of vision deserve to be respected as "contraries"; therefore, they are both "Good" (K 91); both are necessary to "progression" (K 149) in our spiritual life.

Attempts by critics to make the *Songs of Innocence* ironic, to suggest that Blake undercuts or even mocks the perspective and language of innocence, are based on an inadequate grasp of Blake's thought. The state of Innocence, possessed by each of us in childhood or in fantasy, is the proof that we possess the powerful, creative, and Divine Imagination. Experience is, on the other hand, the analytic state of mind that finds the limits of the world that our fallen perception gives us. Both states are "necessary to Human existence" (149), Blake would say; and we must remember that in Blake's thought authentic "Human existence" becomes possible only when we participate in the Divine Humanity in Eternity.

I *Innocence: Pastoralism as Vision*

In the *Songs of Innocence,* pastoralism is the controlling convention; but Blake attains far more with his use of pastoralism than the simplification of relationships that the convention usually achieves. For Blake, the shepherd-sheep relationship and the special world inhabited by shepherd and sheep become the way of representing the characteristic mode of perception in the state of Innocence. Poems

like "The Lamb," "The Shepherd," "The Little Boy Lost/ The Little Boy Found," "A Dream," "Nurse's Song," "A Cradle Song,"
and "On Another's Sorrow" project the innocent's ability to recast
his world imaginatively into one where we can not only be at home
but also be cared for by a loving shepherd. It is pointless to object
that such a world does not exist in what seems to be the world of
common sense and "experience": such an objection would be raised
by a Bacon or by a similar advocate of ratio perception.

The finest poems of the *Songs of Innocence* are those in which
there is some admission of the hardships actually faced by the inno-
cents of the world; but in these poems the innocent view can be seen
as easily transcending adversity. "The Chimney Sweeper" is such a
poem:

> When my mother died I was very young,
> And my Father sold me while yet my tongue
> Could scarcely cry " 'weep! 'weep! 'weep! 'weep!"
> So your chimneys I sweep, & in soot I sleep.
>
> There's little Tom Dacre, who cried when his head,
> That curl'd like a lamb's back, was shav'd: so I said
> "Hush, Tom! never mind it, for when your head's bare
> You know that the soot cannot spoil your white hair."
>
> And so he was quiet, & that very night
> As Tom was a-sleeping, he had such a sight!
> That thousands of sweepers, Dick, Joe, Ned, & Jack,
> Were all of them lock'd up in coffins of black.
>
> And by came an Angel who had a bright key,
> And he open'd the coffins & set them all free;
> Then down a green plain leaping, laughing, they run,
> And wash in a river, and shine in the Sun.
>
> Then naked & white, all their bags left behind,
> They rise upon clouds and sport in the wind;
> And the Angel told Tom, if he'd be a good boy,
> He'd have God for his father, & never want joy.
>
> And so Tom awoke; and we rose in the dark,
> And got with our bags & our brushes to work.
> Tho' the morning was cold, Tom was happy & warm;
> So if all do their duty they need not fear harm. (K 117–18)

We know that the conditions faced by chimney sweepers in the eighteenth century could not have been more inhuman. Tiny, half-starved children died of suffocation or of skin cancer as a result of their lives into which they were indeed "sold." Yet the innocent vision of this poem converts that harsh world into a world of shepherds and sheep: Tom Dacre had white hair as do lambs, and it "curl'd like a lamb's back." When our world cannot support the pastoral vision, Innocence transfers it to an after-life where chimney sweepers will sport like lambs ("down a green hill leaping, laughing they run,/ And wash in a river and shine in the sun") and where they will have a loving father who will be their shepherd ("have God for [a] father, & never want joy").

Clearly, this after-life of a sentimental theology is based on false, or at least irrelevant, moral platitudes ("if all do their duty they need not fear harm"); but it is still an imaginative vision that, experienced by all at times, is proof of our powers. We easily transcend the world of ratio perception, no matter what the claims of the "real world" seem to be. Thus a poem like "The Chimney Sweeper" relies on neither undercutting nor irony: the ability to envision pastoral relationships, despite the world that we presently occupy, is proof of our divinity.

Another fine example of the indomitable character of innocent vision is "The Little Black Boy" in which the horrors of racism and the slave trade, which Blake joined the leaders of the Evangelical movement in opposing, are not ignored but transcended by the vision of the little black boy. His mother's sentimental theology has taught him that " . . . we shall hear his voice,/ Saying: "Come out from the grove, my love & care,/ And round my golden tent like lambs rejoice" " (K 125). And he looks forward to a time " 'When I from black and he from white cloud free,/ . . . round the tent of God like lambs we joy . . .' " (K 125). Again the shepherd-and-sheep relationship replaces the reality of oppression. ". . . he will then love me," the little black boy says; and the word "then" carries the admission of the present relationship between the races. But even so the joyful tone is not undercut, and the innocent vision triumphs.

"Holy Thursday" pictures the charity-children who are brought into St. Paul's on Ascension Day as "multitudes of lambs" who are tended by beadles with "wands as white as snow." Despite the poverty that the children embody, they bring "radiance"; and "like a mighty wind they raise to heaven the voice of song." With the beadles as shepherds, as "wise guardians," they exist happily within the pastoral world of Innocence. A sight such as is presented in this poem seems to justify the pious conclusion "cherish pity lest you drive an angel from your door"; however, outside the perspective of Innocence, Blake argues that, since pity simply accepts existing evils, it is not a virtue.

II *The Mode of Experience: The Analytic Harrow*

Without the perspective of Innocence, we would not be aware of our powers and would remain unable to benefit from what the analysis of the *Songs of Experience* offers us. But, holding the pastoral world of restored relationship and psychological health within us, we are driven toward Eternity when we read "Holy Thursday":

> Is this a holy thing to see
> In a rich and fruitful land,
> Babes reduc'd to misery,
> Fed with cold and usurous hand?
>
> Is that trembling cry a song?
> Can it be a song of joy?
> And so many children poor?
> It is a land of poverty!
>
> And their sun does never shine,
> And their fields are bleak & bare,
> And their ways are fill'd with thorns:
> It is eternal winter there.
>
> For where-e'er the sun does shine,
> And where-e'er the rain does fall,
> Babe can never hunger there,
> Nor poverty the mind appall. (K 211–12)

We know that our life has been cast within an unnatural world, one that is in fact fallen. Thus, in the introduction to *Experience*, the Bard (the Poetic Genius within us) calls to the earth itself:

> "O Earth, O Earth, return!
> Arise from out the dewy grass;
> . . . .
> The starry floor,
> The wat'ry shore,
> Is giv'n thee till the break of day." (K 210)

The heavens, "floored off" by the stars that we think are fixed in their patterns above us, will be opened again by the Divine Imagination. All that prevents our reaching upward and pulling down the heavens with our bare hands, as Los does in *The Four Zoas*, is our diseased mental state that Blake documents mythically in the history of the usurpation of our powers by Urizen. Thus "Earth's Answer" to the Bard:

> "Prison'd on wat'ry shore,
> Starry Jealousy does keep my den:
> Cold and hoar,
> Weeping o'er,
> I hear the Father of the ancient men.
>
> "Selfish father of men!
> Cruel, jealous, selfish fear!
> Can delight,
> Chain'd in night,
> The virgins of youth and morning bear?"
> . . . .
> "Break this heavy chain
> That does freeze my bones around.
> Selfish! vain!
> Eternal bane!
> That free Love with bondage bound." (K 211)

It is the "jealousy" that requires a fixed universe and rigid moral codes that has made the world of our experience an unnatural desert. Urizen, "cold and hoar," "weeping," has caused us to be "chain'd in night" and divorced from the "delight" of energy and Imagination. Quite literally, "free love" would in Blake's view break down the Urizenic universe that is based on law and restraint. As always, Blake stresses the psychological origins of all the suffering that we seem forced to endure in the world of experience.

"The Tyger," Blake's best known poem,[1] is also one of his best accounts of the origins of the limited and terrifying world that we inhabit. "The roaring of lions, the howling of wolves, the raging of the stormy sea, and the destructive sword, are portions of eternity, too great for the eye of man" (K 151), Blake said in *The Marriage of Heaven and Hell*. The mere fact that tigers exist in this world to threaten us is proof of the inadequacy of the world that we conceive. Blake brings the Tyger fully to life before us:

And what shoulder, & what art,
Could twist the sinews of thy heart?
And when thy heart began to beat,
What dread hand? & what dread feet?

What the hammer? what the chain?
In what furnace was thy brain?
What the anvil? what dread grasp
Dare its deadly terrors clasp? (K 214)

The insistent questioning reproduces the very heart beat of the
Tyger and the blows on the anvil struck by the Tyger's creator who
is, of course, the fallen human Imagination that is called Los by
Blake and that is necessarily the source of everything in the world.
"When the stars threw down their spears [their rays]," the creation
was completed in the fixing of "the starry floor." Who then made
the Tyger? We did with our fallen and limited perception that
separates the universe from Eternity and fills a world with threatening objects.

In Eternity, the humanized world of life in the Divine Humanity,
tigers will be seen as men with yellow hair. The result of such a
rehumanization is what Lyca's parents encounter in "The Little Girl
Found" poem of *Experience* when they expect to see a lion:

They look upon his eyes
Fill'd with deep surprise,
And wondering behold
A Spirit arm'd in gold.

On his head a crown,
On his shoulders down
Flow'd his golden hair.
Gone was all their care. (K 114)

When our perception is restored, a human world will surround us
totally. As Blake explains in *Milton,*

These are the Sons of Los, & these the Labourers of the Vintage.
Thou seest the gorgeous clothed Flies that dance & sport in summer
Upon the sunny brooks & meadows: every one the dance
Knows in its intricate mazes of delight artful to weave:
Each one to sound his instruments of music in the dance,
To touch each other & recede, to cross & change & return:

These are the Children of Los; thou seest the Trees on mountains,
The wind blows heavy, loud they thunder thro' the darksom sky,
Uttering prophecies & speaking instructive words to the sons
Of men: These are the Sons of Los: These are the Visions of Eternity,
But we see only as it were the hem of their garments
When with our vegetable eyes we view these wondrous Visions.

(K 512)

Because our vision is only partial, we have closed off such worlds of delight. In "The Little Girl Found," Blake presents the restored world that allows us to see the human lion. He has looked forward to such a restoration in "The Little Girl Lost":

In futurity
I prophetic see
That the earth from sleep
(Grave the sentence deep)

Shall arise and seek
For her maker meek;
And the desart wild
Become a garden mild. (K 112)

"The Little Girl Lost" and "Little Girl Found" pair of poems was appropriately moved from its earlier position in *Innocence:* the poems do look forward to Eternity itself rather than offer the comfort of the innocent vision as does, for instance, "The Chimney Sweeper." Lyca's parents find their lost child not in a pastoral world but in the fully human world of Eternity.

III   *The Deserts of Albion*

The magnificent poem "London" in *Experience* traces the way that our psychological illness has been projected into the kind of institutions of which we are willing parts. Blake's repetitions emphasize the rigid patterning that our perception carries out and the rigid confining trap that we have come to inhabit:

I wander thro' each *charter'd* street,
Near where the *charter'd* Thames does flow,
And *mark in every face* I meet
Marks of weakness, *marks* of woe.

> *In every cry* of *every Man,*
> *In every* Infant's *cry* of fear,
> *In every voice, in every ban,*
> The mind-forg'd manacles I hear. (K 216; italics added)

London, which Blake's myth says should be Jerusalem, has become instead the fullest manifestation of a civilization whose life is based on bad mental habits — on "mind-forg'd manacles."

"Prisons are built with stones of Law, Brothels with bricks of Religion," Blake said in *The Marriage of Heaven and Hell;* and we see in his "London" how the failures of the church and state are made evident through the misery that they cause:

> How the Chimney-sweeper's cry
> Every black'ning Church appalls;
> And the hapless Soldier's sigh
> Runs in blood down Palace walls. (K 216)

The chimney sweeper is blackened by the church that permits children to be sold into this form of slavery; and thus, to any Christian eye, the chimney sweeper blackens the church in return. The state is revealed as the bloody machine of war that it is by Blake's brilliant image of the sigh that turns to blood once it comes in contact with the palace wall. The institution of marriage, because it sets rigid limits on what is permissible sexual behavior, is seen to have contracted the harlot's disease:

> But most thro' midnight streets I hear
> How the youthful Harlot's curse
> Blasts the new born Infant's tear,
> And blights with plagues the Marriage hearse. (K 216)

London has become a black, bloody, and diseased desert because of the mental habits of those who rule it and of those who acquiesce in their rule.

Into a world like that of "London," we must be born in "Infant Sorrow." We are restricted from birth:

> Struggling in my father's hands,
> Striving against my swaddling bands,
> Bound and weary I thought best
> To sulk upon my mother's breast. (K 217)

We suffer as in "The Schoolboy" ("How can the bird that is born for joy/ Sit in a cage and sing?"); and our sexual passions, our impulses toward an apocalyptic freeing by means of love, are checked as in "The Garden of Love":

> I went to the Garden of Love,
> And saw what I never had seen:
> A Chapel was built in the midst,
> Where I used to play on the green.
>
> And the gates of this Chapel were shut,
> And "Thou shalt not" writ over the door;
> So I turn'd to the Garden of Love
> That so many sweet flowers bore;
>
> And I saw it was filled with graves,
> And tomb-stones where flowers should be;
> And Priests in black gowns were walking their rounds,
> And binding with briars my joys & desires. (K 215)

Quite consistently, Blake's imagery for depicting our condition in *Experience* is based on limitation and on restriction, on binding and on enclosure.

"The Chimney Sweeper" in *Experience* now sees through what seems the sentimental escapism of the speaker of "The Chimney Sweeper" in *Innocence:*

> ". . . because I am happy & dance & sing,
> They think they have done me no injury,
> And are gone to praise God & his Priest & King,
> Who make up a heaven of our misery." (K 212)

The happiness of the chimney sweepers is, in fact, without foundation; and their hoped-for escape to a better world is a palliative put together by the alliance of church and state that Blake detested. Blake would have agreed with Soame Jenyns, the amateur theologian of the eighteenth century, who wrote, "impossible it must be that a divine and human Government should subsist together in the same Society, for they must immediately clash; and whenever that happens, the least spark of divine authority, if really divine, must infallibly consume all human power, and destroy all Civil Government whatever."[2] Divine government would mean an end to secular government; therefore, any alliance of priest and king that endures can be seen as having perverted — or killed — whatever was Divine in it.

"The Little Boy Lost" is based on the false hierarchy in love that is often required of us. Blake sees that we must first love the Divine Humanity within ourselves:

> "Nought loves another as itself,
> Nor venerates another so,
> Nor is it possible to Thought
> A greater than itself to know. . . ." (K 218)

For the little boy's refusal to "love" according to institutional prescription, he undergoes the usual punishment of the revolutionary figure (Orc) in Blake's work:

> They strip'd him to his little shirt,
> And bound him in an iron chain;
> And burn'd him in a holy place,
> Where many had been burn'd before:
> The weeping parents wept in vain.
> Are such things done on Albion's shore? (K 218–19)

For Blake, the practice of child sacrifice — whether literal or metaphorical — is the sure sign of a civilization devoted to natural religion. "Are such things done on Albion's shore?" Blake asks. The answer is yes for any land that, virtually by force, turns its children away from what is imaginative and authentic.

Many of the poems in *The Songs of Experience* are written in advocacy of "That free Love" that is presently "with bondage bound." Among these poems, perhaps the best, and certainly the most effectively condensed, is "The Lilly":

> The modest Rose puts forth a thorn,
> The humble Sheep a threat'ning horn,
> While the Lilly white shall in love delight,
> Nor a thorn, nor a threat, stain her beauty bright. (K 215)

The rose's practice of modesty and the sheep's habit of humility disfigure them with "thorn" and "horn." The lily remains unstained because of its spontaneous participation in the "delight" of love. For Blake, modesty and humility are the virtues of those who prefer restraint and secrecy. He denies that Jesus was humble,[3] and he as-

signs "mild humility" to the "sneaking serpent" of the conventionally religious.[4]

IV   *Transcending the Limits of Mortality*

"The Fly," a poem whose meaning has been widely debated,
makes the fundamentally Blakean assertion that all that is real is
mental:[5]

> . . . thought is life
> And strength & breath,
> And the want
> Of thought is death. . . . (K 213)

If this assertion is true, we need not fear death:

> Then am I
> A happy fly,
> If I live
> Or if I die. (K 213)

Similarly, Blake tells us in "To Tirzah" that we need not feel tied to
anything that is mortal:

> Whate'er is Born of Mortal Birth
> Must be consumed with the Earth
> To rise from Generation free:
> Then what have I to do with thee?

"Nature" has limited and warped us:

> Thou, Mother of my Mortal part,
> With cruelty didst mould my Heart,
> And with false self-deceiving tears
> Didst bind my Nostrils, Eyes, & Ears:
>
> Didst close my Tongue in senseless clay,
> And me to Mortal Life betray.

But we are as superior to nature as to mortality: "The Death of Jesus
set me free:/ Then what have I to do with thee?" (K 220).

In "The Fly" and "To Tirzah," we receive Blake's assurance that
experience, the horrors of which would impel us to seek its
transcendence, *can* be transcended. The "world of Imagination is

Infinite & Eternal, whereas the world of Generation, or Vegetation, is Finite & Temporal" (K 605).

V *The Natural Cycle in* The Book of Thel

We find it appropriate to discuss *The Book of Thel* (1789) as a footnote to *The Songs of Innocence and of Experience* because its theme is the passage from Innocence into Experience that we all must undergo. Blake has Enion, one of his mythic characters, lament:

"What is the price of Experience? do men buy it for a song?
Or wisdom for a dance in the street? No, it is bought with the price
Of all that a man hath. . . ." (K 290)

The same idea forms the basis of the headnote to *The Book of Thel:*

Does the Eagle know what is in the pit?
Or wilt thou go ask the Mole?
Can Wisdom be put in a silver rod?
Or love in a golden bowl? (K 127)

The point is simply that wisdom is painfully won by mankind — won by passage through the world of Experience. We have neither "silver rod" nor "golden bowl" but must endure the pains of the senses and the life of the fallen body before winning our way back to Eternity.

Thel is, therefore, a maiden who recognizes, quite rightly, that — although lily, cloud, worm, and clod of clay are satisfied by their roles in nature — mankind is not. The brevity and apparent uselessness of Thel's life moves her to ask for some significant role for herself. But all that she is offered, all that natural man is ever offered, is the opportunity to be food for worms. Her restlessness — her demand for something better — has already caused her to be unsuited for life in the pastoral world of Innocence which, in our lives as fallen men, must end with the recognition that the world we are born into will neither sustain our vision nor answer our demands for personal happiness.

Thel is forced to accept the life of the senses in the physical body:

She saw the couches of the dead, & where the fibrous roots
Of every heart on earth infixes deep its restless twists:
A land of sorrows & of tears where never smile was seen. (K 130)

The natural heart is tied to the natural world to be only a source of torment to us: it is the punishment usually meted out to Orc, who, although he represents our impulse to break down limits, is tied to the physical world in restraint. The "grave" Thel visits is, therefore, her own body:

> . . . waiting oft beside a dewy grave
> She stood in silence, list'ning to the voices of the ground,
> Till to her own grave plot she came, & there she sat down,
> And heard this voice of sorrow breathed from the hollow pit.
>
> "Why cannot the Ear be closed to its own destruction?
> Or the glist'ning Eye to the position of a smile?
> Why are Eyelids stor'd with arrows ready drawn,
> Where a thousand fighting men in ambush lie?
> Or an Eye of gifts & graces show'ring fruits & coined gold?
> Why a Tongue impress'd with honey from every wind?
> Why an Ear, a whirlpool fierce to draw creations in?
> Why a Nostril wide inhaling terror, trembling, & affright?
> Why a tender curb upon the youthful burning boy?
> Why a little curtain of flesh on the bed of our desire?" (K 130)

Thel has no explanation for our anguish and will not pay the price of experience. Instead, she rushes back to the world of Innocence; and the attempt to maintain its perspective in a fallen world is to fall into self-deception. As with "To Tirzah," Blake's point in the brief anecdote of Thel is simply that man can find no satisfaction by means of "nature": he must somehow win his way through it to the sustainable Innocence to be found again in Eternity.

VI Tiriel

Because *Tiriel* (written 1789) employs an earlier attempt at a mythic system, a system whose precise equivalencies have yet to be discovered, we cannot confidently apply what we have learned from our study of *The Book of Urizen* to its events. Instead, we must concur with the *Oxford Companion to English Literature* which says that "the symbolic meaning . . . is obscure."[6] It is clear, nonetheless, that Tiriel represents an image of man that reveals not what Blake calls the Human Form Divine but simply decaying mortality, the life of the flesh that Thel rightly saw can offer us only suffering. Tiriel's sons properly reject such a vision as "unworthy to be call'd the father of Tiriel's race"; Ijim (perhaps an early form of Los) similarly denies that Tiriel can be an accurate image of what man is; and an enchained Zazel (an early version of the revolutionary Orc) throws stones at the unacceptable "Bald tyrant" Tiriel, whose form imprisons energy in restricting flesh.

Tiriel, like Thel, whose story Blake told the same year, first seeks escape from the fact of mortality; he does so by aid of Mnetha (memory) to seek out man's supposed origin in an eternal childhood like the Eden from which conventional Christianity says man fell into mortality. For Blake, the Fall is not, of course, an historical event to be visited by memory; instead, it happens moment by moment as we choose to accept the mortality of Tiriel. Even Tiriel himself, the dying natural body, sees at last the inadequacy of a retreat into a false and sentimental past and ends in a lament much like Thel's. And, like Thel, he has found no way to release the Human Form Divine that resides within him. Blake would have us listen, as Tiriel does not, to the imaginative Ijim and to the passionate Zazel, who refuse to accept the limited conception of man's potential that Tiriel embodies. If we join in such a refusal, we can escape both Thel's fear and Tiriel's. We must learn to say to the merely natural body what Blake said to it in "To Tirzah" in *Songs of Experience:* "Then what have I to do with thee?"

CHAPTER 8

The Four Zoas

O F Blake's long narratives, his *The Four Zoas* written 1797–
1807 is most an "epic" if by that classification we mean a work
on a colossal scale like Milton's *Paradise Lost* or Dante's *Divine
Comedy*. But the subject of *The Four Zoas* is at the same time the
most "personal" of Blake's three epics; for what is depicted, by
means of the gigantic figures of Blake's myth, is the disintegration
and restoration to unity of the faculties that make up the human psy-
che, Blake's and every man's. *The Four Zoas* is the flowering of the
germ of an epic that is in *The Book of Urizen,* and it is probably the
most successful of all the Romantic attempts to turn the epic, usually
concerned with the crucial events in a culture or a faith, into a psychologically oriented form that deals with growth, or at least change,
in consciousness.

Keats's *Hyperion* and *Fall of Hyperion* raise similar themes, but
they remain slim fragments; Wordsworth's *Prelude* is too interested
in the biographical processes by which value is created to achieve
consistently the universality of myth, although moments in the
poem have this power for us; and, though Coleridge's *Ancient
Mariner* is admittedly fully achieved mythic art, its scale is tiny com-
pared to Blake's *Four Zoas*. Thus Blake's poem, chaotic as it is in its
existence as a manuscript with multiple layers of revision, comes
closest to being the Romantic epic that every Romantic poet wanted
to write. Blake's *Milton* and his *Jerusalem* lack this particular kind of
success because of their concern with specific theological, even
"doctrinal," issues.

The Four Zoas was once called *Vala* by Blake, and attempts have
been made to extract this first version from the confused manuscript.
Since it is, however, better critical practice to concentrate on the
latest revised version, we use Geoffrey Keynes's version of the full
poem but follow recent critics in considering the version of "Night

the Seventh" that Keynes prints as the first, as the later one. Of the two titles that Blake considered for the work, certainly the second one, *The Four Zoas*, is the more descriptive since this poem more thoroughly explores the relationships among the faculties — reason (Urizen), energy (Luvah/Orc), the poetic power (Urthona/Los), and integrative perception (Tharmas) — than any of Blake's other works. The Greek word "zoa," actually a plural although Blake used it as a singular, is inadequately translated as "beasts" in the King James version of Revelation; it refers, as we have seen, to the figures — ox, lion, eagle, and man — around the throne of the Lamb. Blake chose not to follow the conventional identification of these figures with the four gospels — or, at any rate, he found the use of them as representatives of the human faculties more productive of the myth that he sought to create.

I The Four Zoas, *"Night the First"*

The Four Zoas is offered as instruction in Vision carried to the point where apocalypse threatens:

. . . long resounding, strong heroic Verse
Marshall'd in order for the day of Intellectual Battle.
The heavens quake, the earth was moved & shudder'd, & the mountains
With all their woods, the streams & valleys wail'd in dismal fear. (K 264)

Such guidance in Vision — disruptive of the fixed world we perceive — Blake means to offer, as a deleted passage tells us, to "whosoever reads/If with his intellect he comprehend." Blake reminds us of the psychological unity from which man has fallen:

Four Mighty Ones are in every Man; a Perfect Unity
Cannot Exist but from the Universal Brotherhood of Eden,
The Universal Man, to Whom be Glory Evermore. Amen. (K 264)

Through Inspiration (mythically through the Daughters of Beulah), he will relate particularly the fall of the prophetic power in us, the fall of Los who is named Urthona in Eternity:

Daughter of Beulah, Sing
His fall into Division & his Resurrection to Unity:
His fall into the Generation of decay & death, & his
Regeneration by the Resurrection from the dead. (K 264)

But the poet will begin with Tharmas, "parent power," a figure that we have not yet encountered in our reading of Blake although he is one of the four zoas that exist in every man.

Tharmas is that impulse toward unified Vision that every man possesses and whose powers are revealed in the state of Innocence. His emanation, his significant creation, is Enion, who should represent unified and flexible perception. But a terrible error has taken place in our mental habits: we no longer recognize what truly unified perception is; we think that order must mean fixity; and with fixity a man's creation is separated from him — as we have seen in *The Book of Urizen*. Thus the emanations of the other zoas, cut off from their creators, flee to Tharmas to seek the order that he should represent. But the very separation of the emanations from the zoas is proof that unified perception is now impossible. Clearly, Tharmas has fallen too — has participated in the fall of the zoas.

As a result of the separation, Tharmas's creation, Enion, stands as a judge over him, just as our inhuman theological or scientific systems are allowed to do. She is now — like the church of Blake's day, like Urizen, and like Satan — an "accuser of sin"; for she advocates "Right & Duty instead of Liberty." Tharmas rightly protests Enion's acts of "jealousy" (to apply Blake's usual word for moral rigidity) and voices the same cry that the eighteenth-century writers such as David Hume had started to raise with the recognition that they lived in a world seemingly alien to them: " 'I am like an atom,/ A Nothing, left in darkness; yet I am an identity:/ I wish & feel & weep & groan. Ah, terrible! terrible!' " (K 265). Yet such an error about the world we inhabit is possible only when we have surrendered our "parent power," when we have forgotten that we create our own environment through the quality of our vision. Thus, as Blake explains mythically, in Eternity "Males immortal live renew'd by female deaths"; that is, emanations do not seek fixity but are content to "revive in spring with music & song" and "in soft/ Delight they die." The products of the Imagination should delight in the seasons of the mind.

Tharmas has fallen by his acquiescence in the fixity of the emanations. Thus, once the "parent power," the principle of order and unity, he sinks into the sea — into the chaotic world of fallen epistemology. And it is the chaos of the material world that Tharmas comes to represent: the chaos that modern atomic theory agrees is beyond the false order that we think we perceive. Enion draws out the specter of Tharmas, all that negates his true principle of unity, to form the perception of those who hold the materialist position. What follows is the warfare between the perceiver and the content of his perception that characterizes man's life in a fallen world:

> The Spectre thus spoke: "Who art thou, Diminutive husk & shell
> Broke from my bonds? I scorn my prison, I scorn & yet I love.
> If thou hast sinn'd & art polluted, know that I am pure
> And unpolluted, & will bring to rigid strict account
> All thy past deeds; hear what I tell thee! mark it well! remember!
> This world is Thine in which thou dwellest; that within thy soul,
> That dark & dismal infinite where Thought roams up & down,
> Is Mine, & there thou goest when with one Sting of my tongue
> Envenom'd thou roll'st inwards to the place whence I emerg'd." (K 268)

Of course, Tharmas is right in knowing that Enion is ultimately subject to him, but he can no longer make her responsive to her creator. Instead, he lives with her in a state of constant bickering like that between any one of us and the environment that we must inhabit.

The coupling of Tharmas, now a principle of materialistic chaos rather than of order, with Enion, the error of inflexible perception, produces time and space — called Los and Enitharmon, respectively, in Blake's myth. That Los and Enitharmon are born in this poem of parents other than those they had in *The Book of Urizen* is not an inconsistency on Blake's part that is worth pausing over since we cannot deny that materialistic habits of mind give birth to these mental categories and in separation from one another. As a result, we can be content with psychological consistency.

Los, despite his prophetic potential, is, like Enitharmon, fully enslaved to the natural heart and its jealousies:

> Alternate Love & Hate his breast: hers Scorn & Jealousy
> In embryon passions; they kiss'd not nor embrac'd for shame & fear.
> His head beam'd light & in his vigorous voice was prophecy.
> He could controll the times & seasons & the days & years;
> She could controll the spaces, regions, desart, flood & forest,
> But had no power to weave the Veil of covering for her sins.
> She drave the Females all away from Los,
> And Los drave the Males from her away. (K 270–71)

Through the chinks of our cavern-minds light can occasionally shine because

. . . Eno, a daughter of Beulah, took a Moment of Time
And drew it out to seven thousand years with much care & affliction
And many tears, & in every year made windows into Eden. (K 270)

Vision, such as the innocent has, stays with mankind to offer some
insight into Eternity. And Infinity still awaits us at either limit:
beyond the universe or within the atom.

   Los understands that Albion would not have fallen had he kept
the Divine Image, Jesus and Man, before him. Thus Los and
Enitharmon's contentions need continue only "Till we have drawn
the Lamb of God into a mortal form," bringing redemption, as it
were, by *means* of time and space. But Enitharmon will not worship
the Divine Image. Instead, to protect her status as a fixed form, she
is prepared to worship Urizen, the god of jealousy and rigidity:

Then Enitharmon, redd'ning fierce, stretch'd her immortal hands:
"Descend, O Urizen, descend with horse & chariot!
Threaten not me, O visionary; thine the punishment.
The Human Nature shall no more remain, nor Human acts
Form the rebellious Spirits of Heaven, but War & Princedom, & Victory &
Blood." (K 272)

Urizen, as always, is willing to appear in this role of seeming
divinity; and he arrives saying, "Now I am God from Eternity to
Eternity." He offers Los power in the fallen world in exchange for
his restraint of Luvah (Orc), who is always the threat to Urizen's
laws and structures. But, when Los is not willing to cooperate,
Urizen suspects the worst:

"Art thou a Visionary of Jesus, the soft delusion of Eternity?
Lo I am God, the terrible destroyer, & not the Saviour.
Why should the Divine Vision compel the sons of Eden
To forego each his own delight, to war against his spectre?
The Spectre is the Man. The rest is only delusion & fancy." (K 273)

The Spectre, all that Blake feels limits a man, *is* man within Urizen's
definition; and Jesus, Who so thoroughly transcends such defini-
tions, must be "the soft delusion of Eternity."

   Los and Enitharmon, time and space, are wed, a repetition of
Tharmas's union with Enion; and, like the previous wedding, theirs
helps to make possible the stony world that we see. Neither time nor
space exists as a category in the healthy mind; and, because Los and
Enitharmon remain separate after their marriage, we can see that

they have simply united to torment us in concert. At the wedding feast, the songs are about the dehumanization that man's world has undergone: " 'The Horse is of more value than the Man. The Tyger Fierce/ Laughs at the Human form; the Lion mocks & thirsts for blood' " (K 275). The refusal of flexibility on the part of Enion and Enitharmon was similar mockery of what is human. Now the very particles of existence, the particles of our perception, refuse the apocalyptic "Plow & Spade, . . . Roller & . . . Harrow" which might be used in "labours of the harvest & the vintage." The energy of Luvah is sealed within these pieces of perception, "The innumerable sons & daughters of Luvah [are] clos'd in furnaces." Our grim desert comes to be the sort of visual environment that we prefer: "There is no City, nor Cornfield, nor Orchard; all is Rock & Sand."

Enion, because she is willing to admit what life in our desert world consists of, can contribute only a lament to the wedding feast:

"Why howl the Lion & the Wolf? why do they roam abroad?
Deluded by summer's heat, they sport in enormous love
And cast their young out to the hungry wilds & sandy desarts.

"Why is the Sheep given to the knife? the Lamb plays in the Sun:
He starts! he hears the foot of Man! he says: Take thou my wool,
But spare my life: *but* he knows not that winter cometh fast." (K 276)

The mental ground has been readied for the inadequate, violent physical world that comes into being with the marriages of Tharmas and Enion and of Enitharmon and Los. Meanwhile, Albion sinks into sleep, watched over by Jesus.

As an appropriate conclusion to "Night the First," the Daughters of Beulah provide us with an account of past disorders within Albion. It seems that Urizen and Luvah, reason and energy, had been in conflict; for both were seeking sovereignty. The dispute frightened Urthona, who permitted Enitharmon to escape from him to Tharmas, a lapse that presumably means that Urthona fell into the mistake of seeking order and permanence in his creations. Enitharmon is "murdered" by Enion; that is, she takes on fixity, what we might call life: "such thing was never known/ In Eden, that one died a death never to be reviv'd."

One result of the disorders in Albion is that Jerusalem, Albion's emanation, is now fallen too; but she is watched over by the Daughters of Beulah, inspiration always remaining to sustain what should be the true faith of Albion. The mental processes of Albion are, by the end of Night One of *The Four Zoas*, the ultimate of solipsism: "His inward eyes closing from the Divine Vision, & all/ His children wandering outside, from his bosom fleeing away" (K 279). Albion's mental condition is that of the empiricist; he is the victim of the same division between perceiver and object of perception. While he is in such a state, there is no possibility of Jerusalem's restoration to him.

II *"Night the Second"*

The destruction of a healthy unified perception, wherein perceiver and object of perception are one, which was Blake's concern in "Night the First," leads necessarily to the fall of the senses into ratio perception that is the subject of the first part of "Night the Second" (which was "Night the First" in *Vala*, Blake's earlier, shorter version of this epic). As "Night the Second" opens, Albion invites Urizen to assume control over his senses:

> "Behold these sick'ning Spheres,
> Whence is this voice of Enion that soundeth in my Porches?
> Take thou possession!" (K 280)

Faced with the chaos that results when we create the material world, Albion joins Urizen in longing for fixity. Urizen is as terrified by the chaos of material vision as Albion is: "He saw the indefinite space beneath & his soul shrunk with horror." But his response is not to flee from materialism but to secure a more rigid form of it,

Petrifying all the Human Imagination into rock & sand.
Groans ran along Tyburn's brook and along the River of Oxford
Among the Druid Temples. Albion groan'd on Tyburn's brook:
Albion gave his loud death groan. The Atlantic Mountains trembled.
Aloft the Moon fled with a cry: the Sun with streams of blood.
. . . .
Jerusalem came down in a dire ruin over all the Earth,
She fell cold from Lambeth's Vales in groans & dewy death. . . . (K 281)

Empiricism, based on a view of the mind that assumes the existence of a material world that is both fixed and independent of us, spreads to the universities ("Oxford/ Among the Druid Temples") and to the Church[1] ("Jerusalem . . . fell cold from Lambeth's Vale"). Ratio perception fixes the Moon "Aloft" and the Sun too. Urizen is creating the "Mundane Shell" seen by all men who take flight from the chaos they themselves create; among the types of his victims are the natural man ("Reuben") and the priest ("Levi"):

Reuben slept on Penmaenmawr & Levi slept on Snowdon.
Their eyes, their ears, nostrils & tongues roll outward, they behold
What is within now seen without; they are raw to the hungry wind. (K 281)

Luvah (Orc), the energy that Urizen fears, is imprisoned within the physical world, "cast into the Furnaces of affliction & sealed." There he is tormented by Vala, properly his emanation, but now the mocking "Nature" that places limits on energy. The suffering Luvah is, however, now fallen too; and he feels that his fall was carried out "to deliver all the sons of God/ From bondage of the Human form." He is, Blake tells us, "Reasoning from the loins in the unreal forms of Ulro's night." His mental powers are perverted by his mistaken materialism.

Ratio perception is established, and only a few men dare question it:

With trembling horror pale, aghast the Children of Man
Stood on the infinite Earth & saw these visions in the air,
In waters & in earth beneath; they cried to one another,
"What! are we terrors to one another? Come, O brethren, wherefore
Was this wide Earth spread all abroad? not for wild beasts to roam."
(K 283)

They ask the proper question — the one that Blake's poem "The Tyger" invites us to ask — in demanding to know why we must inhabit a desert where "wild beasts . . . roam." Most men, however, accept the ratio world, its values, and its forms of life:

But many stood silent, & busied in their families.
And many said, "We see no Visions in the darksom air.
Measure the course of that sulphur orb that lights the darksom day;
Set stations on this breeding Earth & let us buy & sell."
Others arose & schools erected, forming Instruments
To measure out the course of heaven. (K 283)

With "compasses" and "strong scales," their world of fallen vision is meted out to them. The senses (as in the description at the end of

The Book of Thel) become only a torment; for they trap our energies
and close worlds of delight: "In cruel delight they trap the listeners,
& in cruel delight/ Bind them, condensing the strong energies into
little compass" (K 284). But this world, shaped by Urizen in his fear,
is accepted as a comfortable "common-sense" stay by most men;
and we remember Sam Johnson's kicking a stone to refute Bishop
Berkeley.

"Night the Second" concludes with a review of the condition of
the emanations of the four zoas. Earlier (K 282), Luvah has told us
that "Urizen, who was Faith & certainty, is chang'd to Doubt." Accordingly, he is now separated from Ahania, his emanation. Ahania
would represent wisdom if Urizen still possessed her, and Vala
would represent fulfilled emotional life. Instead, Vala finds herself
in torment like that of the women in *Visions of the Daughters of Albion:* " 'We are made to turn the wheel for water,/ To carry the
heavy basket on our scorched shoulders. . . .' " (K 285–56).
Enitharmon should represent the creative acts of Los, but she mocks
him instead as the threatening space that the artist must overcome:
" ' . . . for thou art mine,/ Created for my will, my slave, tho' strong,
tho' I am weak' " (K 288). And Enion, who should represent fulfilled
perception, is now trapped within the vision of Experience:

"What is the price of Experience? do men buy it for a song?
Or wisdom for a dance in the street? No, it is bought with the price
Of all that a man hath, his house, his wife, his children.
Wisdom is sold in the desolate market where none come to buy,
And in the wither'd field where the farmer plows for bread in vain." (K 290)

In the cries of the four "females," we find a full sense of what the
shattering of our vision of Eternity has cost us.

III   *"Night the Third"*

"Night the Third" is the shortest of the sections that make up *The
Four Zoas,* and it consists primarily of a flashback narrative that is
provided by Ahania who is speaking to Urizen. Urizen rightly fears
that he cannot forever sustain the mundane shell that he caused to
be created for ratio perception; but Ahania reminds him of his rise to
power over Albion. Albion, because of his "wearied intellect," has,
in effect, deified Urizen, the rational faculty — a process repeated
by the thinkers of the Enlightenment or by any man envisioning a
lawmaker God:

Idolatrous to his own Shadow, words of Eternity uttering:
"O I am nothing when I enter into judgment with thee.
If thou withdraw thy breath I die & vanish into Hades;
If thou dost lay thine hand upon me, behold I am silent;
If thou withhold thine hand I perish like a fallen leaf.
O I am nothing, & to nothing must return again.
If thou withdraw thy breath, behold I am oblivion." (K 293)

The idea of holiness has been externalized by Albion, who forgets that all deities reside in the human breast. The result of the deification of the rational faculty is the rejection of the energetic: "Then frown'd the Fallen Man [Albion] & put forth Luvah from his presence." Rejected energy petrifies into the deceptive natural heart:

. . . Luvah and Vala
Went down the Human Heart, where Paradise & its joys abounded,
In jealous fears, in fury & rage, & flames roll'd round their fervid feet,
And the vast form of Nature like a Serpent play'd before them. . . . (K 294)

A healthy emotional life is replaced by the torments of jealousy.

But Urizen finds no comfort in hearing again how he was elevated and how Luvah was demoted. He is still fearful; and his separated emanation, Ahania, his own "wisdom," now reflects only his own weakness: " '. . . thou hast risen with thy moist locks into a wat'ry image/ Reflecting all my indolence, my weakness & my death . . .' " (K 295). He casts her off: a despairing suicidal act that the rational mind was often driven to in the eighteenth century and afterwards. We think especially of Lord Byron, the Romantic poet who, through characters like Cain and Manfred, most strongly expressed man's resentment at the limited scope that our knowledge of the world offers us; but Byron rejected all possibility of wisdom found through the Imagination by saying that it only reveals how "Of its own beauty is the mind diseased,/ And fevers into false creation."

With the separation of Ahania from Urizen, Tharmas, who should represent our unified perception, has completed his metamorphosis into the total chaos represented by the sea, the best emblem of the chaotic "atomic" world we choose to inhabit. Tharmas's voice is now blubbering confusion:

"My skull riven into filaments, my eyes into sea jellies
Floating upon the tide wander bubbling & bubbling,

Uttering my lamentations & begetting little monsters
Who sit mocking upon the little pebbles of the tide
In all my rivers & on dried shells that the fish
Have quite forsaken. O fool! fool! to lose my sweetest bliss." (K 296)

Enion, who should be the world that is seen by unified perception, longs to return to Tharmas; but he cannot repossess the healthy state of vision that he once had:

"Why does thy piteous face Evanish like a rainy cloud
Melting, a shower of falling tears, nothing but tears! Enion,
Substanceless, voiceless, weeping, vanish'd, nothing but tears! Enion,
Art thou for ever vanish'd from the wat'ry eyes of Tharmas?" (K 297)

The clear, definite vision of Eternity has been replaced by the watery vistas of ratio perception and by the material world it creates. There is only Urizen's fear to suggest that anything could undo his fallen world.

IV   "Night the Fourth"

In "Night the Fourth," Los, the "prophetic boy" (K 292) who is feared by Urizen, is forced to put his Imagination into the service of ratio perception and ultimately to give shape to Urizen as ruler of this world. Tharmas starts this process by producing from the division of Los and Enitharmon the Spectre of Urthona who represents everything that limits the imaginative poet. The Spectre of Urthona responds to the threats that are most destructive of the artist who would transcend this world. Thus Tharmas gains his obedience through terrifying him with images of death: " 'If thou refusest, dash'd abroad on all/ My waves, thy limbs shall separate in stench & rotting, & thou/ Become a prey to all my demons of despair & hope' " (K 299).

The poet who hears these threats responds by seeking the false order of, let's say, a British eighteenth-century poet. Fear, originating in the fallen natural heart, drives Los into fixing the creations of Urizen as he did in the *Book of Urizen* (and indeed Blake borrows most of his description of the process from that work). Thus even art has been rendered subservient to a false epistemology, and the artist seems a correspondingly lessened figure: "[Los] became what he beheld:/ He became what he was doing: he was himself transform'd" (K 305). The process was called Neo-Classicism in literary history.

But the fall has reached its limits at this point — although specific solidifications of error like Natural Religion and "Nature" itself are yet to appear. Jesus has set limits in every man's psychology beyond which he cannot fall: the limits are necessarily there, of course, since men, despite their fallen nature, are innately Divine. Thus:

The Saviour mild & gentle bent over the corse of Death,
Saying, "If ye will Believe, your Brother shall rise again."
And first he found the Limit of Opacity, & nam'd it Satan,
In Albion's bosom, for in every human bosom these limits stand.
And next he found the Limit of Contraction, & named it Adam,
While yet those beings were not born nor knew of good or Evil. (K 304)

Men will not perceive a world more opaque, more closed to Eternity, than that which Urizen now gives us. (Urizen's fallen name is, of course, Satan, the god of this world and the Accuser of Sin.) Men will not shrink beyond the forms our bodies now possess: we will not fall ("contract") beyond the state reached by Adam. From this base at least, Los — though now a victim of the Spectre of Urthona, his own fears — can work for renewal.

V   "Night the Fifth"

"Night the Fifth" pictures the binding of energy within the natural world that is, at the same time, the entry of apocalyptic hope into our world of time and space. As the Daughters of Beulah had said at the end of "Night the Fourth," Jesus appears "cloth'd in Luvah's garments that we may behold [Him] / And live." Los and Enitharmon, separated and petrified, "Shrunk into fixed space . . . unexpansive," live in the darkness and cold of a Urizenic world. Into this winter season Luvah (Orc) is born as was Jesus at Christmas. But, as always, Luvah-Orc is the revolutionary power; he represents energy that demands its rightful place in our mental universe, and is such a threat that his own parents must resist him. He enacts what we, long after Blake, have come to see as a fundamental act of adolescent rebellion:

But when fourteen summers & winters had revolved over
Their solemn habitation, Los beheld the ruddy boy
Embracing his bright mother, & beheld malignant fires
In his young eyes, discerning plain that Orc plotted his death.
Grief rose upon his ruddy brows; a tightening girdle grew
Around his bosom like a bloody cord; in secret sobs

He burst it, but next morn another girdle succeeds
Around his bosom. Every day he view'd the fiery youth
With silent fear. . . . (K 307)

Los is bound in the girdle of jealousy, which means not simply sexual
jealousy, but the fear of the loss of order that jealousy is based upon.
Orc's very presence may be seen as "warring with the waves of
Tharmas & Snows of Urizen" and as, therefore, a threat to the Los
who, in "Night the Fourth," "became what he beheld." As in *The
Book of Urizen*, Los chains Orc, thereby tying him to the natural cycle, an act which means that now only the violent harrowing that
destroys the "physical" can bring about our return to Eternity (as it
does in the later books of *The Four Zoas*). In the process from which
Thel fled, Orc has the torments of the natural heart:

Lo, the young limbs had stucken root into the rock, & strong
Fibres had from the Chain of Jealousy inwove themselves
In a swift vegetation round the rock & round the Cave
And over the immortal limbs of the terrible fiery boy.
In vain they strove now to unchain, In vain with bitter tears
To melt the chain of Jealousy. . . . (K 309)

The howling of the energetic Orc for freedom shakes the world and
hints at apocalypse: "Urizen trembled . . . to hear the howling terror" (K 310).

Urizen now regrets the loss of Eternity and offers a weary lamentation (K 310–11). But he must nevertheless set out to assess the
threat represented by the shaking of the world by the furious Luvah-
Orc: " 'I will arise, Explore these dens, & find that deep pulsation/
That shakes my cavern with strong shudders; perhaps this is the
night/ Of Prophecy, & Luvah hath burst his way from Enitharmon' " (K 311). "Night the Sixth" offers the record of his quest.

VI   *"Night the Sixth"*

At the outset of "Night the Sixth," Urizen encounters "three terrific women," who turn out to be his own daughters. Most commen-
tators take them to be representative of the loins, the heart, and the
brain. If this identification is the right one for each of these, they
should represent the visionary potential carried in our lives by sex,
emotion, and Imagination; and, not surprisingly, Urizen offers them
"chains," "cords," and "whips" for an enslavement like that en-

dured by the Daughters of Albion "that they may worship terrors & obey the violent" (K 313). When we see these women again, they are (like Vala) tormenters of Orc and are the repressors of energy through their advocacy of Moral Virtue.

Next, Urizen encounters Tharmas, who is in such a state of despair over the quality of his perception that he seeks a death pact with Urizen:

"The Body of Man is given to me. I seek in vain to destroy,
For still it surges forth in fish & monsters of the deeps,
And in these monstrous forms I Live in an Eternal woe,
And thou, O Urizen, art fall'n, never to be deliver'd.
Withhold thy light from me for ever, & I will withhold
From thee thy food; so shall we cease to be, & all our sorrows
End, & the Eternal Man no more renew beneath our power." (K 313)

Since there is no body distinct from the soul, as Blake has told us, Tharmas, as keeper of Man's body, is the custodian of perception. Yet Tharmas's perception is like ours; it is full of unaccountable outbreaks of energy ("fish & monsters of the deeps") that should tell us that we have imposed a false order on the world. Urizen, who simply ignores Tharmas's pleas and threats, seeks for himself further abstractions with which to close the gaps in perception of which Tharmas complains. As a first step, Urizen, like a good empiricist, investigates the condition of mankind:

Scar'd at the sound of their own sigh that seems to shake the immense
They wander Moping, in their heart a sun, a dreary moon,
A Universe of fiery constellations in their brain,
An earth of wintry woe beneath their feet, & round their loins
Waters or winds or clouds or brooding lightnings & pestilential plagues.
Beyond the bounds of their own self their senses cannot penetrate:
As the tree knows what is outside of its leaves & bark
And yet it drinks the summer joy & fears the winter sorrow. . . . (K 314)

Falsely closed within themselves, men find only sorrow. Yet there are everywhere proofs of the inadequacy of their solipsistically formed universe: "Then he beheld the forms of tygers & of Lions, dishumaniz'd men." A human world awaits each of us outside the caverns into which we have closed ourselves.

Urizen tries to conduct the sort of apocalyptic questioning that Blake's "The Tyger" would urge us to undertake: "Oft would he stand & question a fierce scorpion glowing with gold;/ In vain; the terror heard not" (K 315). Urizen doesn't know how to pursue such a quest for truth: the empirical method yields no real answers to the "Idiot Questioner" who employs it. Since Urizen cannot free mankind ("He could not take their fetters off. . . ."), he creates scientific explanations of its condition, "Creating many a Vortex, fixing many a Science in the deep." Like the true empiricist, like Bromion in *Visions of the Daughters of Albion*, he longs for better conditions of "observation":

But Urizen said: "Can I not leave this world of Cumbrous wheels,
Circle o'er Circle, nor on high attain a void
Where self sustaining I may view all things beneath my feet?
Or sinking thro' these Elemental wonders, swift to fall,
I thought perhaps to find an End, a world beneath of voidness
Whence I might travel round the outside of this dark confusion." (K 316–17)

He is certain that, given the right sort of laboratory conditions, he can explain our anguish to us. For, as post-Newtonian man soon knew, our world seems only the ruins of Paradise:

"O what a world is here, unlike those climes of bliss
Where my sons gather'd round my knees! O, thou poor ruin'd world!
Thou horrible ruin! once like me thou wast all glorious,
And now like me partaking desolate thy master's lot." (K 317)

He creates bigger abstractions, fancier systems:

So he began to form of gold, silver & iron
And brass, vast instruments to measure out the immense & fix
The whole into another world better suited to obey
His will, where none should dare oppose his will, himself being King
Of All, & all futurity be bound in his vast chain.
And the Sciences were fix'd & the Vortexes began to operate
On all the sons of men, & every human soul terrified
At the turning wheels of heaven shrunk away inward, with'ring
    away. (K 317)

"A living Mantle adjoined to his life & growing from his soul," his new science stretches as "the Web of Urizen." He has spun out explanations of all that he sees and sits at the center a grim and hoary spider.

Finally, the empiricist approaches the possible gap in his web represented by the fierce Orc whose anguish first started Urizen on his scientific quest. But Urizen cannot now approach Orc, for even such demented characters as Tharmas and the Spectre of Urthona intervene to protect him. Instead, as "Night the Sixth" ends, Urizen retreats to his scientist's spider web where the planets whirl about him:

Then Urizen arose upon the wind, back many a mile
Retiring into his dire Web, scattering fleecy snows:
As he ascended, howling loud, the Web vibrated strong,
From heaven to heaven, from globe to globe. In vast excentric paths
Compulsive roll'd the Comets at his dread command, the dreary way
Falling with wheel impetuous down among Urthona's vales
And round red Orc; returning back to Urizen, gorg'd with blood.
Slow roll the massy Globes at his command, & slow o'erwheel
The dismal squadrons of Urthona weaving the dire Web
In their progressions, & preparing Urizen's path before him. (K 319–20)

We have filled our heads with webs like these, and we use them to "see" the sky with. But such systems still do not account for the possible eruption of Luvah-Orc — or for the coming of Jesus.

VII "*Night the Seventh*," *Revised Version*

As Geoffrey Keynes points out, "Blake wrote two versions of Night the Seventh, but did not finally reject either" (K 320). The version printed first by Keynes as having been written earlier, but considered by recent scholars to be the later in date of composition, moves from the preceding "Night the Sixth" with the more natural transition and introduces concepts of considerable value for our understanding of the concluding nights of *The Four Zoas*. It begins with Urizen's rising from his solipsistic web of stars to look into another's flaming rich bosom, the act that Orleans summoned us to in *The French Revolution* as an antidote for our desire to be lawgivers. This kingdom is Orc's:

But Urizen silent descended to the Caves of Orc & saw
A Cavern'd Universe of flaming fire; the horses of Urizen
Here bound to fiery mangers, furious dash their golden hoofs,
Striking fierce sparkles from their brazen fetters fierce his lions
Howl in the burning dens; his tygers roam in the redounding smoke
In forests of affliction; the adamantine scales of justice
Consuming in the raging lamps of mercy, pour'd in rivers.

The holy oil rages thro' all the cavern'd rocks; fierce flames
Dance on the rivers & the rocks; howling & drunk with fury
The plow of ages & the golden harrow wade thro' fields
Of goary blood; the immortal seed is nourish'd for the slaughter.
The bulls of Luvah, breathing fire, bellow on burning pastures
Round howling Orc, whose awful limbs cast forth red smoke & fire,
That Urizen approach'd not near but took his seat on a rock
And rang'd his books around him, brooding Envious over Orc. (K 320)

What Urizen sees, of course, is a world of pure energy, energy of a
sort that consumes Urizenic "scales of justice" and threatens to
bring out the plow and harrow that will tear apart Urizen's ratio-
perception world. But, since Orc is himself in fetters, Urizen can
safely sit to watch his torments.

Urizen's jealousy, which has already wrought so many evils, is
now the parent of the Tree of Mystery which represents all religions
that repress energy and Imagination. Orc, who is forced to circle this
tree, assumes the serpent form of priestcraft (see, for instance, *The
French Revolution*) as a punishment for his continuing assertions to
Urizen that his "fierce fires are better than [Urizen's] snows." The
daughters of Urizen hold Orc, always a potentially revolutionary
energy, by the arts of "Moral Virtue" that serve only to support
privilege:

"Compell the poor to live upon a Crust of Bread, by soft mild arts.
Smile when they frown, frown when they smile; & when a man looks pale
With labour & abstinence, say he looks healthy & happy;
And when his children sicken, let them die; there are enough
Born, even too many, & our Earth will be overrun
Without these arts. If you would make the poor live with temper,
With pomp give every crust of bread you give; with gracious cunning
Magnify small gifts; reduce the man to want a gift, & then give with pomp.
Say he smiles if you hear him sigh. If pale, say he is ruddy.
Preach temperance: say he is overgorg'd & drowns his wit
In strong drink, tho' you know that bread & water are all
He can afford. Flatter his wife, pity his children, till we can
Reduce all to our will, as spaniels are taught with art." (K 323)

Through such arts Orc is transformed, against his will, to serve
Urizen as a priest so "that he might draw all human forms/ Into submission to his will."

Los has, in the meantime, lost Enitharmon whose shadow now
flees to the Tree of Mystery to start the process by which a world

perceived as "space" can be joined to the idea of religion and form a natural religion. Urizen had wished that his daughters might "Draw down Enitharmon to the Spectre of Urthona,/ And let him have dominion over Los," and he seems to be having his way as Enitharmon and the Spectre of Urthona mate at the Tree of Mystery to bring into being Vala who will ultimately be the full embodiment of natural religion. (In mental terms, such union and birth mean that all that limits the Imagination has merged with a false concept of space to produce the assumptions behind the characteristic theology of the eighteenth century.) But Urizen doesn't get his way entirely; for the Spectre of Urthona, who reveals his own sense of inadequacy in his conversation with Enitharmon, offers to join with Los in producing visionary works of art:

"If we unite in one, another better world will be
Open'd within your heart & loins & wondrous brain,
Threefold, as it was in Eternity, & this, the fourth Universe,
Will be Renew'd by the three & consummated in Mental fires; . . . (K 329)

The works they produce together will be only threefold, subject to the limits of opacity and contraction ("having a Limit Twofold nam'd Satan & Adam"); but they will bring the Imagination to the borders of Eternity again.

Enitharmon tries to introduce doubt into Los's mind by arguing for "accusation of sin" and the doctrine of the atonement, "That without a ransom I could not be sav'd from Eternal death." But Los is now too strong to accept these deceptions from the Tree of Mystery. He can even provide the Blakean response: " 'Turn inwardly thine Eyes & there behold the Lamb of God Clothed in Luvah's robes of blood descending to redeem' " (K 330). Clearly he is ready to take on the role of visionary artist; and, as he does, so he compels even the cooperation of the recalcitrant spatial world: "And first he drew a line upon the walls of shining heaven,/ And Enitharmon tinctur'd it with beams of blushing love./ It remain'd permanent, a lovely form, inspir'd, divinely human" (K 332).

Such works of art are produced for our benefit, and they serve as "counterparts" for our visionary yearnings that otherwise have no outlet. And Blake's own art, clearly suggested here by the drawing of the visionary line and by the subsequent coloring of the outline, has the same intention. These products of the Imagination are loved by Los, who refuses "to Sacrifice their infant limbs"; and he, with

Blake, is now ready to lead us toward the apocalypse through the concluding nights of *The Four Zoas*. Already, in fact, his art has transformed all that is fearful in Urizen into the easily recognizable figure of Satan; and, though finding "his Enemy Urizen now in his hands," Los can feel "love & not hate." Soon all the energy that Urizen (now Satan) feared at the outset of "Night the Seventh" will be released.

VIII   *"Night the Eighth"*

"Night the Eighth" of *The Four Zoas* is centrally concerned with the fall of the English church into the delusions of natural theology, but it simultaneously depicts the renewed presence of Jesus in the hearts of the Inspired. As a result, this section is the historical prelude to the apocalypse that Blake saw about him in his own time. There are signs of Albion's awakening as "Night the Eighth" opens:

> Man began
> To wake upon the Couch of Death; he sneezed seven times;
> A tear of blood dropped from either eye; again he repos'd
> In the Saviour's arms, in the arms of tender mercy & loving kindness.
>
>   (K 341)

Los is again able to "behold the Divine Vision" through the stony fallen world that we must inhabit. And Enitharmon now labors to provide the "counterparts" of visionary art for men like us who have fallen into single vision.

Urizen is driven to a final effort by these new threats to his realm. With the connivance of priestcraft ("Communing with the Serpent of Orc in dark dissimulation"), he creates the totally solipsistic vision that his self-enclosure has always tended toward:

> . . . a Shadowy hermaphrodite, black & opake;
> The soldiers nam'd it Satan, but he was yet unform'd & vast
> Hermaphroditic it at length became, hiding the Male
> Within as in a Tabernacle, Abominable, Deadly. (K 343)

The confusion between "perceiver" and "perceived" that characterizes the empirical method results in a hermaphrodite world that confuses the "man" and his emanation. Los resists the formation of such a world, closed as it would be to vision, and struggles to humanize its particles:

They humanize in the fierce battle, where in direful pain
Troop by troop the beastial droves rend one another, sounding loud
The instruments of sound; & troop by troop, in human forms, they urge
The dire confusion till the battle faints; those that remain
Return in pangs & horrible convulsions to their beastial state;
For the monsters of the Elements, Lions or Tygers or Wolves,
Sound loud the howling music Inspir'd by Los & Enitharmon, sounding
   loud; terrific men
They seem to one another, laughing terrible among the banners. (K 344)

The imperfect process of humanization leads, as always, to the formation of terrifying tigers and other "monsters" who are the proof of the inadequacy of our vision. These terrors form Urizen's world:

And Urizen gave life & sense by his immortal power
To all his Engines of deceit: that linked chains might run
Thro' ranks of war spontaneous: & that hooks & boring screws
Might act according to their forms by innate cruelty.
He formed also harsh instruments of sound
To grate the soul into destruction, or to inflame with fury
The spirits of life, to pervert all the faculties of sense
Into their own destruction, if perhaps he might avert
His own despair even at the cost of every thing that breathes. (K 344)

This world is the painful one of the senses from which Thel fled but in which the empiricist delights.

Vala, our knowledge of the natural world, takes on the "enormous Sciences of Urizen" to become the scientific world view of the eighteenth century. Then she is wed to "the tree of Mystery" to become, completely and at last, natural religion. Meanwhile, the imaginative acts of all fallen men ("the dead") take shape as Jerusalem:

And Enitharmon named the Female, Jerusalem the holy.
Wond'ring, she saw the Lamb of God within Jerusalem's Veil;
The Divine Vision seen within the inmost deep recess
Of fair Jerusalem's bosom in a gently beaming fire. (K 346)

From Jerusalem will come Jesus to overthrow "the dark Satanic body" whose formation we have seen.

Satan acts to protect himself and to counter the efforts of the

Imagination. One method he relies on is the identification of all that
is visionary as sin: "to . . . reveal/ Naked of their clothing the poor
spectres before the accusing heavens." To replace the visionary garments, he brings "webs of torture,/ Mantles of despair, girdles of
bitter compunction, shoes of indolence,/ Veils of ignorance"; and all
of these are too often the garb of those suffering under the weight of
imputed sin. All their anguish contributes to the preservation of
natural religion: " ' . . . this Lake is form'd from the tears & sighs &
death sweat of the Victims/ Of Urizen's laws, to irrigate the roots of
the tree of Mystery' " (K 347). Satan is now all that opposes or seeks
to negate Jerusalem, "Being multitudes of tyrant Men in union
blasphemous/ Against the Divine image, Congregated assemblies of
wicked men." But he can be no match for Jesus, Who is willing to
work through the Satanic world — "Assume the dark Satanic body
in the Virgin's womb" — and to bring it to Apocalypse.

A corrupt institutionalized religion (Rahab) and the natural world
(Tirzah) on which it is founded assert their power over Jesus in the
Crucifixion:

Thus was the Lamb of God condemn'd to Death.
They nail'd him upon the tree of Mystery, weeping over him
And then mocking & then worshipping, calling him Lord & King.
Sometimes as twelve daughters lovely, & sometimes as five
They stood in beaming beauty, & sometimes as one, even Rahab
Who is Mystery, Babylon the Great, the Mother of Harlots. (K 349)

Jerusalem, who should represent the vital faith of Albion, mis-
interprets the Crucifixion and gives birth to a religion which is a cult
of death:

" . . . let us build
A Sepulcher & worship Death in fear while yet we live:
Death! God of All! from whom we rise, to whom we all return:
And Let all Nations of the Earth worship at the Sepulcher
With Gifts & Spices, with lamps rich emboss'd, jewels & gold." (K 349)

At first, Los also misunderstands and, "despairing of Life Eternal,"
buries Jesus.

But Los recovers his sight quickly, recognizes Rahab for what she
is, and offers the history of the fall of man to demonstrate his
visionary understanding. Urizen meanwhile petrifies as a result of
his petrified vision, "his human form a Stone,/ A form of Senseless

Stone remain'd. . . ." Tharmas and Urthona turn over their respective "Power" and "Strength" to Los, who will carry on their
apocalyptic strivings for them. Ahania and Enion return to lament
man's fallen condition again, but Enion looks forward to the
humanization of the universe:

> "The Lamb of God has rent the Veil of Mystery, soon to return
> In Clouds & Fires around the rock & the Mysterious tree.
> And as the seed waits Eagerly watching for its flower & fruit,
> Anxious its little soul looks out into the clear expanse
> To see if hungry winds are abroad with their invisible army,
> So Man looks out in tree & herb & fish & bird & beast
> Collecting up the scatter'd portions of his immortal body
> Into the Elemental forms of every thing that grows." (K 355)

All the principals have gathered for the tremendous finale that Blake
has prepared. Natural Religion takes on the precise historical
character that it had when Blake wrote this poem: Jerusalem is
"Captive . . . by delusive arts impell'd/ To worship Urizen's Dragon
form, to offer her own Children/ Upon the bloody Altar." Rahab,
cast into defining flames, becomes a Phoenix of Error: "The Ashes of
Mystery began to animate; they call'd it Deism/ And Natural
Religion; as of old, so now anew began/ Babylon again in Infancy,
call'd Natural Religion" (K 357). Error has now been identified; and
Los, the imaginative artist, is, like Blake, ready to counter it.

IX "*Night the Ninth*"

"Night the Ninth" of *The Four Zoas* returns us at last to Eternity.
The process begins when Los, still mourning the apparent loss of
Jesus to the sepulcher, experiences the fear that is Vision:

> Terrified at Non Existence,
> For such they deem'd the death of the body, Los his vegetable hands
> Outstretch'd; his right hand, branching out in fibrous strength,
> Siez'd the Sun; His left hand, like dark roots, cover'd the Moon,
> And tore them down, cracking the heavens across from immense to im-
> mense. (K 357)

What Los does here is what any man could do if he would. And,
because he has proved man's superiority over "space" and "time,"
the Spectre of Enitharmon and the Spectre of Urthona also fall and
have "Their bodies buried in the ruins of the Universe. . . ."

Urizen's books unroll, and the serpent Orc "began to Consume in fierce raving fire. . . ."

The Last Judgment is at once under way because, as Blake said elsewhere, "Whenever any Individual Rejects Error & Embraces Truth, a Last Judgment passes upon that Individual" (K 613). When Los, our imaginative faculty, refuses to accept the Newtonian world, we are lifted toward Eternity: ". . . from the clotted gore & from the hollow den/ Start forth the trembling millions into flames of mental fire,/ Bathing their limbs in the bright visions of Eternity" (K 358). The institutions that had been founded upon a fallen epistemology come at once to an end: tyrants lose their power, and the Tree of Mystery is immediately consumed. And at last Albion comes fully awake.

Albion is now clear-sighted enough to castigate Urizen, now a stony dragon, for his errors. Urizen responds at once by rejecting the jealous mental habit that had tried to control "futurity" by making laws:

"Then Go, O dark futurity! I will cast thee forth from these
Heavens of my brain, nor will I look upon futurity more.
I cast futurity away, & turn my back upon that void
Which I have made; for lo! futurity is in this moment." (K 361–62)

With this act, he frees himself of his long characteristic "snows" and "his aged mantles":

Then, glorious bright, Exulting in his joy,
He sounding rose into the heavens in naked majesty,
In radiant Youth; when Lo! like garlands in the Eastern sky
When vocal may comes dancing from the East, Ahania came
Exulting in her flight, as when a bubble rises up
On to the surface of a lake, Ahania rose in joy. (K 362)

The union with Ahania is somewhat premature since the final humanization of the world has not yet taken place; but Ahania *will* soon be restored to the reborn Urizen.

As the Universe humanizes, the once oppressive Newtonian shapes are seen for what they are — as the body of Satan that crucifies Jesus and as the corrupters of theology. Thus they begin to reform as well: "They see him whom they have pierc'd, they wail because of him,/ They magnify themselves no more against Jerusalem" (K 364). Every man's perception is improving.

Luvah and Vala return to the loins of Albion where they belong;
and Tharmas and Enion are restored to the pastoral world of Innocence that healthy perception once knew, a fit world for "the
lovely eyes of Tharmas & the Eyes of Enion." Thus any aspect of our
vision that had seemed at all unpleasant is now filled with joy:

> The roots shoot thick thro' the solid rocks, bursting their way
> They cry out in joys of existence; the broad stems
> Rear on the mountains stem after stem; the scaly newt creeps
> From the stone, & the armed fly springs from the rocky crevice,
> The spider, The bat burst from the harden'd slime, crying
> To one another: "What are we, & whence is our joy & delight?
> Lo, the little moss begins to spring, & the tender weed
> Creeps round our secret nest." Flocks brighten the Mountains,
> Herds throng up the Valley, wild beasts fill the forests. (K 373)

And it is Tharmas, restored perception, who can announce the end
of the religions based on false epistemology and point to the eradication of the social evils that those religions wrought: "Mystery is no
more" (K 375).

The physical world that we have known undergoes a crushing into
"Human Wine" as all the zoas, now their Eternal selves, join in the
work. And Eternity is present again:

> The Sun has left his blackness & has found a fresher morning,
> And the mild moon rejoices in the clear & cloudless night,
> And Man walks forth from midst of the fires: the evil is all consum'd.
> His eyes behold the Angelic spheres arising night & day;
> The stars consum'd like a lamp blown out, & in their stead, behold
> The Expanding Eyes of Man behold the depths of wondrous worlds!
> One Earth, one sea beneath; nor Erring Globes wander, but Stars
> Of fire rise up nightly from the Ocean; & one Sun
> Each morning, like a New born Man, issues with songs & joy
> Calling the Plowman to his Labour & the Shepherd to his rest.
> He walks upon the Eternal Mountains, raising his heavenly voice.
> Conversing with the Animal forms of wisdom night & day,
> That, risen from the Sea of fire, renew'd walk o'er the Earth,
> For Tharmas brought his flocks upon the hills, & in the Vales
> Around the Eternal Man's bright tent, the little children play
> Among the wooly flocks. The hammer of Urthona sounds
> In the deep caves beneath; his limbs renew'd, his Lions roar
> Around the Furnaces & in Evening sport upon the plains.
> They raise their faces from the Earth, conversing with the Man. (K 379)

This fully human world of restored perception resembles the pastoral world of Innocence, but it is now not to be threatened by our entry into Experience. The once terrifying sun is human, "a New born Man," and the Lions we once feared now chat with us. The life of mortal warfare is done with, and there is now only the pleasure of "intellectual war," the art and science of Eternity: "The war of swords departed now,/ The dark religions are departed & sweet Science reigns" (K 379). "The dark Religions" which spoke of atonement and the accusation of sin are now replaced by vision. Man has awakened to his own divinity.

CHAPTER 9

Manuscript Poems

THE poetry of Blake that remained unpublished and unillumi-
nated included not only the epic *The Four Zoas* but also a large
number of shorter manuscript poems that are both lyric and satiric.
Some of these are indeed variants of poems used in *Innocence* or
Experience or elsewhere, but a few have long earned a place of their
own in collections of Blake's poetry. One of the best known is Blake's
fierce rejection of Voltaire and Rousseau — and of all materialistic
and empirical science:

> Mock on, Mock on Voltaire, Rousseau:
> Mock on, Mock on: 'tis all in vain!
> You throw the sand against the wind,
> And the wind blows it back again.
>
> And every sand becomes a Gem
> Reflected in the beams divine;
> Blown back they blind the mocking Eye,
> But still in Israel's paths they shine.
>
> The Atoms of Democritus
> And Newton's Particles of light
> Are sands upon the Red sea shore,
> Where Israel's tents do shine so bright. (K 418)

There is as well the defiantly shapeless "Auguries of Innocence,"
which offers a strong statement of Blake's view that a recognition of
the inadequacies of the world we inhabit is a summons to Vision and
reminds us that "We are led to Believe a Lie/ When we see not
Thro' the Eye" (K 433). But neither of these poems makes the demand for attention in its own terms that is made by each of three

mysterious cyclical poems that appear in what is called "The Pickering Manuscript" after its Victorian owner, B. M. Pickering.

The best clue to the meaning of these three manuscript poems — "The Golden Net," "The Mental Traveller," and "The Crystal Cabinet" — lies in that cyclical structure itself. The poems, probably written about 1803 when Blake was still involved with *The Four Zoas,* concern the deceptive natural cycle to which we enslave ourselves when we submit to the promptings of the natural heart. Through the repetition of phrase or incident, Blake creates striking counterparts to the "mills," the great circles that enclose us within our skulls, within time, and within this universe.

I   *"The Golden Net"*

In "The Golden Net," a "young Man" feels pity rather than fury at the plight of three maidens whose visionary garments contain an entire history of repression:

> The one was Cloth'd in flames of fire,
> The other Cloth'd in iron wire,
> The other Cloth'd in tears & sighs. . . . (K 424)

Desire ("fire") and its restraint ("iron wire") will result in "tears & sighs" unless an apocalyptic solution is offered. The young man has none and is, as a result, enslaved himself by virtue of the pity that the natural heart within him has felt. The maidens spread a net over him:

> Underneath the Net I stray,
> Now intreating Burning Fire,
> Now intreating Iron Wire,
> Now intreating Tears & Sighs. (K 424)

The repetitions enforce the point, underlining the presence of the cyclical trap. "O when will the morning rise?," the young man wonders; but he has himself insured that the morning of Vision remains far off.

II   *"The Mental Traveller"*

The most challenging of the cyclic poems is the difficult "The Mental Traveller" in which the repetitions seem to be the most mocking. The speaker of the poem is a "mental traveller" who will offer a visionary account of life in our fallen world, the world of

Generation ("A Land of Men & Women too"). We are told how Nature — Tirzah in Blake's myth — repeats the binding of Orc in every man's life, giving him the suffering natural heart in the process:

> She binds iron thorns upon his head,
> She pierces both his hands & feet,
> She cuts his heart out at his side
> To make it feel both cold & heat. (K 425)

It is this heart that leads a man first to sexual love and then to the practice of the fallen virtue of pity, a virtue only possible when we *accept* an inadequate world. Pity is often institutionalized into charitable organizations:

> An aged Shadow, soon he fades,
> Wand'ring round an Earthly Cot,
> Full filled all with gems & gold
> Which he by industry had got.
>
> And these are the gems of the Human Soul,
> The rubies & pearls of a lovesick eye,
> The countless gold of the akeing heart,
> The martyr's groan & the lover's sigh.
>
> They are his meat, they are his drink;
> He feeds the Beggar & the Poor
> And the wayfaring Traveller:
> For ever open is his door. (K 425)

But such institutions cannot endure the birth of a new concept such as that represented by "A little Female Babe":

> And she is all of solid fire
> And gems & gold, that none his hand
> Dares stretch to touch her Baby form,
> Or wrap her in his swaddling-band. (K 425)

The infant Orc, victim of Nature, is now the ancient Urizen: thus creative "male" and "female" creation are always out of phase in the world of Generation.

The reaction that the Urizenic figure brings into being, an analogue to political reaction, destroys even the charitable institutions to leave us face to face with the desert of ratio perception:

> The Senses roll themselves in fear,
> And the flat Earth becomes a Ball;
>
> The stars, sun, Moon, all shrink away,
> A desart vast without a bound.
> And nothing left to eat or drink,
> And a dark desart all around. (K 426)

Yet, on the other hand, because a new idea has come into being, the Urizenic figure becomes rapidly more youthful until he is again the infant Orc who is not yet victim to the ancient abstraction "Nature":

> . . . he becomes a wayward Babe,
> And she a weeping Woman Old.
> Then many a Lover wanders here;
> The Sun & Stars are nearer roll'd. (K 426)

The world becomes momentarily more human as lovers walk in freedom again and as the stars cease to be quite so remote as they usually are. But reaction is inevitable:

> They cry "The Babe! the Babe is Born!"
> And flee away on Every side.
>
> For who dare touch the frowning form,
> His arm is wither'd to its root;
> Lions, Boars, Wolves, all howling flee,
> And every Tree does shed its fruit.
>
> And none can touch that frowning form,
> Except it be a Woman Old;
> She nails him down upon the Rock,
> And all is done as I have told. (K 427)

There is no hope of human satisfaction — or of a human life at all — within the natural cycle. Political change is meaningful only as it represents our movement toward apocalypse. If political faiths are based on an acceptance of the natural cycles, based on an empirical epistemology, they too will fail. Our happiness is to be found only when we can shatter all the enclosing wheels of nature and time.

III   *"The Crystal Cabinet"*

If "The Mental Traveller" offers hints about the impossibility of success in merely political endeavor, "The Crystal Cabinet" offers a clear warning against a reliance on sexuality to lead to transcendence of our condition. In this poem, the speaker encounters a maiden who seems to be able to offer him entry into a realm which is, somehow, this physical world repeated in a finer tone:

> She put me into her Cabinet
> And Lock'd me up with a golden Key.
>
> The Cabinet is form'd of Gold
> And Pearl & Crystal shining bright,
> And within it opens into a World
> And a little lovely Moony Night.
>
> Another England there I saw,
> Another London with its Tower,
> Another Thames & other Hills,
> And another pleasant Surrey Bower. . . . (K 429)

Could he possess her here he might possess a Keatsian — or Lawrentian — eternity:

> . . . like a flame I burn'd;
> I bent to Kiss the lovely Maid,
> And found a Threefold Kiss return'd. (K 429)

But his attempt must fail, and his actual subservience to nature is underlined:

> I strove to seize the inmost Form
> With ardor fierce & hands of flame,
> But burst the Crystal Cabinet,
> And like a Weeping Babe became —
>
> A weeping Babe upon the wild,
> And Weeping Woman pale reclin'd,
> And in the outward air again
> I fill'd with woes the passing Wind. (K 429–30)

Nature is to be destroyed or transcended. Its "inmost Form," could it be grasped, provides only the grounds for the despair of the empiricist.

These three cyclical poems offer a particularly effective statement against trusting either a political revolution or a sexual one as a final answer. Blake advocated both kinds of revolution but only as a first step toward the full freedom of Eternity. "Many persons, such as Paine & Voltaire, with some of the Ancient Greeks, say: 'we will not converse concerning Good & Evil; we will live in Paradise & Liberty.' You may do so in Spirit, but not in the Mortal Body as you pretend, till after the Last Judgment . . ." (K 615–16). The trap that Paine or Voltaire creates in accepting nature is reproduced in the structure of these poems: nature's seasons or the alternations of revolution and counter-revolution enclose us, as do the tight patterns of repeated incident and repeated phrase. The three cyclical poems, taken together with the other manuscript poems, remind us that, even though Blake chose to devote much of his career to works on a larger scale, he had few peers in the fusion of form and meaning in the short poem.

CHAPTER 10

Milton

IN *Milton* (c. 1810), Blake returns to his quarrel with the last major epic poet in English. As Blake told us in *The Marriage of Heaven and Hell*, Milton, despite his own energy and imagination, chose to picture a rational and bloodless Jesus. But, if we are to be restored to Eternity, emotion and inspiration must be returned to their rightful place in both art and religion. If Blake's *Jerusalem* is concerned with the English church's turning from accusation to forgiveness of sin, his *Milton* argues for that church's return to prophecy and Imagination. Thus Blake's Preface pleads that "the Daughters of Memory shall become the Daughters of Inspiration."

To this end, the rational Greek and Roman thinkers must no longer be set up against "the Sublime of the Bible," an attitude with which the Milton of *Paradise Regained* concurred. We must instead, as artists and Christians, be "just & true to our own imaginations, those Worlds of Eternity in which we shall live for ever in Jesus our Lord." When this truth is achieved, then Jerusalem, the art and religion — the "emanation" — of Albion can be restored to a land now dominated by the "mills" of Newtonian thought. Blake's magnificent lyric, now usually entitled "Jerusalem," completes the Preface:

> And did those feet in ancient time
> Walk upon England's mountains green?
> And was the holy Lamb of God
> On England's pleasant pastures seen?
>
> And did the Countenance Divine
> Shine forth upon our clouded hills?
> And was Jerusalem builded here
> Among these dark satanic Mills?

> Bring me my Bow of burning gold:
> Bring me my Arrows of desire:
> Bring me my Spear: O clouds unfold!
> Bring me my Chariot of fire.
>
> I will not cease from Mental Fight
> Nor shall my Sword sleep in my hand
> Till we have built Jerusalem
> In England's green & pleasant Land. (K 480-81)

This poem has long been a "hymn" of the British Labour Party, but it is just as appropriately a hymn of the Church of England. It is Blake's call for a restored, non-"natural," non-rational theology. "Would to God," Blake pleads, "that all the Lord's people were prophets."

I   *"Book the First"*

Milton, because he was a prophet to the English, must share much of the blame for the present state of English theology with the arch-villains, Bacon, Newton, and Locke. *Milton* recounts, therefore, that poet's own return to Imagination and his joining Blake in opposition to the Daughters of Memory, mere rationality, and the concomitant ratio perception:

> Daughters of Beulah! Muses who inspire the Poet's Song,
> Record the journey of immortal Milton thro' your Realms
> Of terror & mild moony lustre in soft sexual delusions
> Of varied beauty, to delight the wanderer and repose
> His burning thirst & freezing hunger! Come into my hand,
> By your mild power descending down the Nerves of my right arm
> From out the Portals of my brain, where by your ministry
> The Eternal Great Humanity Divine planted his Paradise,
> And in it caus'd the Spectres of the Dead to take sweet forms
> In likeness of himself. Tell also of the False Tongue! vegetated
> Beneath your land of shadows, of its sacrifices and
> Its offerings: even till Jesus, the image of the Invisible God,
> Became its prey, a curse, an offering and an atonement
> For Death Eternal in the heavens of Albion & before the Gates
> Of Jerusalem his Emanation, in the heavens beneath Beulah. (K 481)

Milton's penitential passage through Beulah, the realm where emanations rest from the Intellectual Wars of Eternity, and hence the realm where the events of any myth "exist," is simply his entry into a world created by an artist tied to Generation. (All fallen art is "sexual delusion," but such an identification is not really harsh criticism of it. We shall at last transcend both the sexes and the need for media in art; but, until then, we welcome "sexual delusion" not as a refuge from Eternity but as a genuine improvement over the anguish of life in Generation.) The degeneration of Christianity into natural religion with its Druid "sacrifices" and with a Jesus subject to the law in an "atonement" will be among Blake's other subjects in this poem. Blake himself will write from the dictation of "The Eternal Great Humanity Divine," which, thanks to the Daughters of Inspiration, is easily accessible in the minds of all the Lord's people.

Milton has of course passed to Eternity as one of "the Elect," as the Calvinist sects would say; but Blake can imagine what Milton's response to the authentic art of Eternity would have to be. He would necessarily receive the sort of instruction in Vision that each of Blake's plates is intended to provide. Thus Milton's errors are revealed to him by his hearing in Eternity "A Bard's Prophetic Song," a Blakean visionary epic in miniature. Indeed, it offers a capsule version of *The Book of Urizen* in its description of the creation of the fallen forms of man (K 482–83). But, although that fundamental error in perception is the source of all our woes, Blake's special emphasis for the instruction of the vision of John Milton must be the usurpation of the role of inspiration by reason. Thus the Bard's song recounts how Satan, "Newton's Pantocrator, weaving the woof of Locke," gained the use of the "fiery Harrow" of art and religion from Palamabron, who is a true artist and, like Los, is often identified with Blake himself. This story is based on the same tragic confusion about human powers of which, Blake would say, *Paradise Lost* offers the "history." Once Milton hears the events, told in the clear outlines of mythic art, he will be compelled to cast off error: thus the Bard can well say to him, "Mark well my words! they are of your eternal salvation." (K 482)

The Satan of the Bard's song is not only a fallen Urizen, the embodiment of ratio perception and Law, but also the most admired type of man in the systems that are born of such perception. Thus, when Los is compelled as usual to fix the changes of Urizen, he is also driven to create three classes of men who are called by Urizenic religion the Elect, the Redeemed, and the Reprobate. The Elect are those who benefit from "Offering & Atonement in the cruelties of Moral Law" and who, like Satan, depend on the accusation of sin and are exalted in a religion of Druid sacrifices such as Blake felt natural religion to be. The other two classes are the "Redeemed" who are seen in Blake's work as those seeking redemption like ourselves, and the "Reprobate," whom the religious might consider to be devils but who are actually the fiery prophets whom we repress both in our society and in our own personalities.

Lambeth, seat of the Church of England, lies metaphorically in ruins and is now a source of the "Oak Groves" and "Druid Temples" of natural religion:

. . . Lambeth's Vale
Where Jerusalem's foundations began, where they were laid in ruins,
Where they were laid in ruins from every Nation, & Oak Groves rooted,
Dark gleams before the Furnace-mouth a heap of burning ashes.
When shall Jerusalem return & overspread all the Nations?
Return, return to Lambeth's Vale, O building of human souls!
Thence stony Druid Temples overspread the Island white,
And thence from Jerusalem's ruins, from her walls of salvation
And praise, thro' the whole Earth were rear'd. . . . (K 485–86)

From what was once, and will again be, the foundation of Jerusalem in England, faulty perception based on faulty psychology spreads its cancer.

Satan interferes with the harrow of art, just as the church has allowed ratio perception to intrude upon inspiration. He cannot manage it, of course, just as rational inquiries into Christianity bring only despair. And similarly Palamabron cannot keep the sober order that Satan's mills require:

Los beheld
The servants of the Mills drunken with wine and dancing wild
With shouts and Palamabron's songs, rending the forests green
With ecchoing confusion. . . . (K 488)

In the contention that follows, Theotormon and Bromion, familiar to us as the mistaken accusers of sin in the *Visions of the Daughters of Albion,* support Satan while Rintrah, the wrathful prophet of *The Marriage of Heaven and Hell,* opposes him.

An assembly is called to judge; but, as happened in Milton's bifurcation of Jesus into two men, one rational and one energetic, and in the church's drift toward natural religion, the blame falls — quite unfairly — on the prophet Rintrah. With this result, Satan is free to denounce Palamabron, to promulgate his moral laws, and to assert his dominance: " 'I am God alone:/ There is no other! let all obey my principles of moral individuality' " (K 490). And, historically, and perhaps in part because of the prophet Milton, men now "worship Satan under the Unutterable Name." Within our civilization, Satan's victory is best seen in the depression of art and inspiration and in the dominance of natural religion. The doctrine of atonement replaces the forgiveness of sins: "one must die for another throughout all Eternity" (K 491).

Leutha, "a Daughter of Beulah" but frequently associated with feelings of guilt as in *Visions of the Daughters of Albion*, recognizes Satan's error and tries to take the blame herself for it. She sees Satan's crime as a longing for the life of art inspired by her own love for Palamabron, but such confusion of roles is possible only because of an earlier fall: "The Sin was begun in Eternity and will not rest to Eternity." Despite her plea, the stonification of the world is finished; the prophets become the Reprobate: Jesus Himself "died as a Reprobate, he was Punish'd as a Transgressor" (K 494). British theology sinks into the mire of empiricism: "In dreams [Leutha] bore Rahab, the mother of Tirzah, & her sisters/ In Lambeth's vales, in Cambridge & in Oxford, places of Thought." And here the Bard, who has sung "According to the inspiration of the Poetic Genius/ Who is the eternal all-protecting Divine Humanity," ends his song.

The Bard enters Milton's bosom, indicating thereby his having achieved total communication with him. Milton immediately realizes that he has been mistaken to wear "the robe of the promise" as one of the Elect. He will return to life ("Eternal Death") to try to bring an end to the errors he once helped gain a footing in England. He will try to restore his emanation to himself, an emanation that is now as separate from him, he realizes, as Jerusalem is from Albion. He realizes that he has shared the solipsism of empirical perception, creating a hermaphroditic form for man: ". . . he beheld his own Shadow/ A mournful form double, hermaphroditic, male & female/ In one wonderful body . . ." (K 496). Thus Milton returns to earth, entering Blake's left foot.

As Milton returns to corporeal life, his real body, the spiritual one, remains in Eternity. Thus it is only Milton's shadow that will walk again on Earth (just as it is only the shadow of his eternal individuality that leads the corporeal life of any man). He passes the vortices of other universes, perceiving them as spheres because he is not within them; but he does not enter the vortex of Earth, which he can perceive as it is, as the "one infinite plain" that the perception of

every man shows it to be. (Thus Blake would assert that the earth
was flat.) Milton locates his biographical emanation, his three wives
and three daughters who are locked in Ulro and are frozen abstractions rather than the dynamic participants in Jerusalem that they
might be. Still ready to take dictation, they surround him; and they
ask that he be their Moses, his body the "Rock Sinai" from which he
will promulgate the Puritan vision. But Milton leaves them; instead,
he enters the London that Los strives to make visionary but that is
bound in the bands of natural religion.

Los is frightened by Milton's appearance, particularly since
Enitharmon exults that he has come so that "Satan shall be unloos'd
upon Albion." Indeed, the natural world seems to rejoice at Milton's
return because it seems it will now be enthroned as the basis for a
system of natural religion from which there is no appeal:

And thus the Shadowy Female howls in articulate howlings:
"I will lament over Milton in the lamentations of the afflicted:
My Garments shall be woven of sighs & heart broken lamentations:
The misery of unhappy Families shall be drawn into its border,
Wrought with the needle with dire sufferings, poverty, pain & woe
Along the rocky Island & thence throughout the whole Earth;
There shall be the sick Father & his starving Family, there
The Prisoner in the stone Dungeon & the Slave at the Mill.
I will have writings written all over it in Human Words
That every Infant that is born upon the Earth shall read
And get by rote as a hard task of a life of sixty years.
I will have Kings inwoven upon it & Councellors & Mighty Men:
The Famine shall clasp it together with buckles & Clasps,
And the Pestilence shall be its fringe & the War its girdle
To divide into Rahab & Tirzah that Milton may come to our tents.
For I will put on the Human Form & take the Image of God,
Even Pity & Humanity, but my Clothing shall be Cruelty,
And I will put on Holiness as a breastplate & as a helmet,
And all my ornaments shall be of the gold of broken hearts,
And the precious stones of anxiety & care & desperation & death
And repentance for sin & sorrow & punishment & fear,
To defend me from thy terrors, O Orc, my only beloved!" (K 499)

Virtues of the natural heart will replace real humanity, and
"Holiness" will be entirely allied with warfare. All that is energetic
and imaginative will be repressed through conceptions of "sin." Orc
tries to resist, but his efforts only lead to the appearance of Urizen,
who is as stony and as icy as ever.

But Milton's return has not been understood. He has heard the

Bard's song, he has realized that the Puritan Milton was "Satan," and a new Milton has been born who counters Urizen's attempt to inflict the icy baptism of rationality on his head:

> . . . with cold hand Urizen stoop'd down
> And took up water from the river Jordan, pouring on
> To Milton's brain the icy fluid from his broad cold palm.
> But Milton took of the red clay of Succoth, moulding it with care
> Between his palms and filling up the furrows of many years,
> Beginning at the feet of Urizen, and on the bones
> Creating new flesh on the Demon cold and building him
> As with new clay, a Human form in the Valley of Beth Peor. (K 500)

Milton will force Urizen to be Human rather than allow his own achieved Humanity to be Urizenic again. Since Succoth is the place to which Jesus went after the Crucifixion, Milton is trying to shape Urizen into the resurrected Humanity. Milton's emanations, aspects of the emanation of the Puritan Milton, are traitors to the cause of the Imagination; but they have already been identified as Rahab and Tirzah, natural religion and delusive nature, who sing the praises of natural religion, who offer to sacrifice Jerusalem, and who assert the superiority of nature to Jesus:

> "Where is the Lamb of God? where is the promise of his coming?
> Her shadowy Sisters form the bones, even the bones of Horeb
> Around the marrow, and the orbed scull around the brain.
> His images are born for War, for Sacrifice to Tirzah,
> To Natural Religion, to Tirzah, the Daughter of Rahab the Holy!" (K 501)

They offer Milton the position to which he in some sense aspired in setting out to be England's great epic poet: they offer him the kingship of "Canaan," a false promised land woven of rationality and nature; but Milton now serves only Albion, who begins to awaken.

Milton knows now how to view the seemingly frozen natural world that our bad perception gives us. He knows, as does Blake, that "the little winged fly . . . has a heart like thee, a brain open to heaven and hell" and that all that alien world of fierce animals and cold stone is human. He would now say with Blake:

> Seek not the heavenly father then beyond the skies,
> There Chaos dwells & ancient Night & Og & Anak old.
> For every human heart has gates of brass & bars of adamant

Which few dare unbar, because dread Og & Anak guard the gates
Terrific: and each mortal brain is wall'd and moated round
Within, and Og & Anak watch here: here is the Seat
Of Satan in its Webs: for in brain and heart and loins
Gates open beneath Satan's Seat to the City of Golgonooza,
Which is the spiritual fourfold London in the loins of Albion. (K 502)

Indeed, since Milton has entered Blake's foot, his restored vision is
one with Blake's. Blake sees the world as totally humanized, as a
mere sandal for that visionary foot: "all this Vegetable World appear'd on my left Foot/ As a bright sandal form'd immortal." And
the imaginative Milton will soon be reunited with his proper emanation, Ololon, who represents what might have been had Milton's
theology not been tainted with rationality and the law. Ololon,
uniting with Jesus and thus representing a restored theology, pre-
pares to descend to be reunited with Milton.

Not only does Milton combine with Blake, but Los does too. The
union occurs in Lambeth, where Jerusalem's foundations once were
and where they will again be if natural theology can be overcome.
Rintrah and Palamabron, sons of Los, at first fear Milton because
they understand that he has contributed significantly to the es-
tablishment of the erroneous views of the natural theologian:

"And all the Daughters of Los prophetic wail; yet in deceit
They weave a new Religion from the new Jealousy of Theotormon.
Milton's Religion is the cause: there is no end to destruction.
Seeing the Churches at their Period in terror & despair,
Rahab created Voltaire, Tirzah created Rousseau,
Asserting the Self-righteousness against the Universal Saviour,
Mocking the Confessors & Martyrs, claiming Self-righteousness,
With cruel Virtue making War upon the Lamb's Redeemed
To perpetuate War & Glory, to perpetuate the Laws of Sin.
They perverted Swedenborg's Visions in Beulah & in Ulro
To destroy Jerusalem as a Harlot & her Sons as Reprobates,
To raise up Mystery the Virgin Harlot, Mother of War,
Babylon the Great, the Abomination of Desolation." (K 506)

They do know that the Evangelical movement has provided hints of
a return to imaginative religion:

"But then I rais'd up Whitefield, Palamabron rais'd up Westley,
And these are the cries of the Churches before the two Witnesses.
Faith in God the dear Saviour who took on the likeness of men,

Becoming obedient to death, even the death of the Cross.
The Witnesses lie dead in the Street of the Great City:
No Faith is in all the Earth: the Book of God is trodden under Foot.
He sent his two Servants, Whitefield & Westley: were they Prophets,
Or were they Idiots or Madmen? shew us miracles!
Can you have greater Miracles than these? Men who devote
Their life's whole comfort to intire scorn & injury & death?
Awake, thou sleeper on the Rock of Eternity! Albion awake!" (K 506)

But Rintrah and Palamabron do not recognize that Milton aids
rather than hinders the work begun by the Evangelicals. Los pleads
for a kind of ecumenism that would include Milton too: " 'Remember how Calvin and Luther in fury premature/ Sow'd War
and stern division between Papists & Protestants./ Let it not be so
now! O go not forth in Martyrdoms & Wars!' " (K 507). Los remains
"The Watchman of Eternity," the inspired prophet; and he can see
Milton as "the Signal that the Last Vintage now approaches."

The restoration of humanity can begin now that Milton is free
from the shackles of natural religion. And Blake's concern in what
remains of "Book the First" of *Milton* is to demonstrate what
"nature" really is. All the particles of the created world will be
crushed in the "Wine-press" of Vision when we tear to bits the
frozen Urizenic world that we had thought it necessary to inhabit.
Change will begin in Lambeth with the expulsion of natural religion
from the church:

". . . you shall Reap the whole Earth from Pole to Pole, from Sea to Sea,
Beginning at Jerusalem's Inner Court, Lambeth, ruin'd and given
To the detestable Gods of Priam, to Apollo, and at the Asylum
Given to Hercules, who labour in Tirzah's Looms for bread,
Who set Pleasure against Duty, who Create Olympic crowns
To make Learning a burden & the Work of the Holy Spirit, Strife:
The Thor & cruel Odin who first rear'd the Polar Caves.
Lambeth mourns, calling Jerusalem: she weeps & looks abroad
For the Lord's coming, that Jerusalem may overspread all Nations." (K 511)

We can tear apart the physical world, or do with it what we will,
when we come to see it as what it is — fully a product of the
Imagination. Thus everything we perceive is born of Los:

These are the Children of Los; thou seest the Trees on mountains,
The wind blows heavy, loud they thunder thro' the darksom sky,
Uttering prophecies & speaking instructive words to the sons

Of men: These are the Sons of Los: These the Visions of Eternity,
But we see only as it were the hem of their garments
When with our vegetable eyes we view these wondrous Visions. (K 512)

Ratio perception has closed these worlds of delight, but they can be
opened again.

Similarly, the barriers seemingly provided by time are only creations of Los. For the prophet, there has always been human time to
break through the sequence of hours:

Every Time less than a pulsation of the artery
Is equal in its period & value to Six Thousand Years,
For in this Period the Poet's Work is Done, and all the Great
Events of Time start forth & are conciev'd in such a Period,
Within a Moment, a Pulsation of the Artery. (K 516)

In any case, what we call Time is a special gift of Los's; it "is the
mercy of Eternity" because it is, in fact, speeding toward
apocalypse.

The so-called "Science" of a Newton, on which natural religion
was built, is replaced on these last few plates of "Book the First" of
Milton by "the Science of the Elohim," which makes it evident that
everything is holy. Blake asserts that "every Natural Effect has a
Spiritual Cause . . . for a Natural Cause only seems" (K 513). He
mocks the "Microscope" and the "Telescope" (as he did in the case
of the super-empiricist Bromion) because they only "alter/ The ratio
of the Spectator's Organs." In truth:

. . . every Space larger than a red Globule of Man's blood
Is visionary, and is created by the Hammer of Los:
And every Space smaller than a Globule of Man's blood opens
Into Eternity of which this vegetable Earth is but a shadow. (K 516)

Infinity awaits us in either direction — as every twentieth-century
scientist knows.

With the improved epistemology of Milton, natural religion is
robbed of one of its pillars, the belief in "nature." The church can
begin to be reborn in Lambeth, and this vegetable world can cease
to screen off Eternity. If Milton can now embrace his proper emanation — he has rejected all that was mistaken — Jerusalem can
analogously be restored to Albion. Then "all the Lord's people" can
be "Prophets."

II *"Book the Second"*

In "Book the Second," Ololon, Milton's true emanation and therefore a sound art and theology, descends into Beulah, the usual refuge for emanations. And because Beulah, land of inspiration, does "terminate in rocky Albion," because even the stony world of Generation has art as a window onto the truth, the residents of "all Nations" can now see "the Lord coming/ In the clouds of Ololon with Power & Great Glory." "War" — that is "Not Mental, as the Wars of Eternity" — dominates fallen mankind; but the lamentation of Beulah over Ololon, who is still not restored to Milton, challenges men with inspired beauty as does the song of birds or the odor of flowers: the sense of what is missing in our lives is spreading, and "Men are sick with Love."

Milton no longer has any sympathy for "The idiot Reasoner" who "laughs at the Man of Imagination." His immortal part, still in Eternity as is the visionary part of each of us, hears the instruction of "the Seven Angels of the Presence" who warn against Satan and against judging Individuals rather than the States that they are in. But "The Imagination is not a State: it is the Human Existence itself." We hear the Divine Vision calling for the restoration of Jerusalem whose place in Albion has been usurped by Babylon, and we are instructed in the levels of "Humanity in its Repose" — beneath dynamic Eternity — which are called Beulah, Alla, Al-Ulro, and Or-Ulro, a systemization of the levels of Vision not found in this precise form elsewhere in Blake.

After all this information has been imparted — all of it imaginative and valuable — Ololon has even more reason to lament the world men now inhabit; for it is "a frozen bulk subject to decay & death" (K 525). Perhaps our situation appears to the Eternals even worse than it really is since, not having undergone incarnation, they do not see the hope that is created even by the generation-bound artist:

. . . they
Could not behold Golgonooza without passing the Polypus,
A wondrous journey not passable by Immortal feet, & none
But the Divine Saviour can pass it without annihilation.
For Golgonooza cannot be seen till having pass'd the Polypus
It is viewed on all sides round by a Four-fold Vision,
Or till you become Mortal & Vegetable in Sexuality,
Then you behold its mighty Spires & Domes of ivory & gold. (K 525)

But Ololon will, as Milton did earlier, risk annihilation to descend to earth. She finds one of the gaps in time that we have considered before:

There is a Moment in each Day that Satan cannot find,
Nor can his Watch Fiends find it; but the Industrious find
This Moment & it multiply, & when it once is found
It renovates every Moment of the Day if rightly placed.
In this moment Ololon descended to Los & Enitharmon. . . . (K 526)

Ololon, who had been "multitudes" before, can now, having entered the Polypus, be seen as "A Virgin of twelve years." She appears to Blake in Felpham, the location of the cottage in which he worked as an artist "To display Nature's cruel holiness, the deceits of Natural Religion."

Ololon will be Milton's emanation, so now, to complete the usual division of a man in Blake's system, we get a full vision of Milton's Spectre (K 527–30). This specter, a compound of all forms of natural religion, is the Covering Cherub that keeps us from Paradise. Ultimately, he is that Satan who has bound "Jerusalem . . . in chains in the Dens of Babylon." Milton knows that Satan is his Spectre (K 529) and is ready to cast off all that belongs to the "Natural Heart." Satan resists and asks deification as "God the judge of all." With this stark opposition, the tension has reached a breaking point. Albion, England, is reanimated; and the giant figure Albion walks, gaining particular support from the cathedral cities:

London & Bath & Legions & Edinburgh
Are the four pillars of his Throne: his left foot near London
Covers the shades of Tyburn: his instep from Windsor
To Primrose Hill stretching to Highgate & Holloway.
London is between his knees, its basements fourfold;
His right foot stretches to the sea on Dover cliffs, his heel
On Canterbury's ruins; his right hand covers lofty Wales,
His left Scotland; his bosom girt with gold involves
York, Edinburgh, Durham & Carlisle, & on the front
Bath, Oxford, Cambridge, Norwich; his right elbow
Leans on the Rocks of Erin's Land, Ireland, ancient nation.
His head bends over London. . . . (K 531)

Ololon feels that she cannot face the full embodiment of evil that the times have wrought: " '. . . this thing, this Newtonian Phantasm, /

This Voltaire & Rousseau, this Hume & Gibbon & Bolingbroke,/
This Natural Religion, this impossible absurdity . . .' " (K 532).
    But Milton's total espousal of the imaginative leads to the state-
ment that is ultimately to console Ololon, destroy Satan, and restore
Jerusalem to Albion:

"I come in Self-annihilation & the grandeur of Inspiration,
To cast off Rational Demonstration by Faith in the Saviour,
To cast off the rotten rags of Memory by Inspiration,
To cast off Bacon, Locke & Newton from Albion's covering,
To take off his filthy garments & clothe him with Imagination,
To cast aside from Poetry all that is not Inspiration,
That it no longer shall dare to mock with the aspersion of Madness
Cast on the Inspired by the tame high finisher of paltry Blots
Indefinite, or paltry Rhymes, or paltry Harmonies,
Who creeps into State Government like a catterpiller to destroy;
To cast off the idiot Questioner who is always questioning
But never capable of answering, who sits with a sly grin
Silent plotting when to question, like a thief in a cave,
Who publishes doubt & calls it knowledge, whose Science is Despair,
Whose pretence to knowledge is envy, whose whole Science is
To destroy the wisdom of ages to gratify ravenous Envy
That rages round him like a Wolf day & night without rest:
He smiles with condescension, he talks of Benevolence & Virtue,
And those who act with Benevolence & Virtue they murder time on time.
These are the destroyers of Jerusalem, these are the murderers
Of Jesus, who deny the Faith & mock at Eternal Life,
Who pretend to Poetry that they may destroy Imagination
By imitation of Nature's Images drawn from Remembrance.
These are the Sexual Garments, the Abomination of Desolation,
Hiding the Human Lineaments as with an Ark & Curtains
Which Jesus rent & now shall wholly purge away with Fire
Till Generation is swallowed up in Regeneration." (K 533)

The full Blakean faith is in these lines which begin with the replace-
ment of the Daughters of Memory by the Daughters of Inspiration
and which move to a restored Jerusalem and to Jesus's triumph over
nature.
    Ololon enters the breast of the Milton who now speaks fully from
Inspiration. And the world is ready for apocalypse: ". . . clouds roll
over London with a south wind; soft Oothoon/ Pants in the Vales of
Lambeth, weeping o'er her Human Harvest" (K 535). Oothoon, the
spirit of America and thus as representative of Liberty as Jerusalem,

is returned to Lambeth. The wine presses will begin their work of restoring the frozen particles of our world to visionary ones. ". . . terrific Lions & Tygers" seem bursting with the portions of Eternity that they contain. And here, abruptly, Blake's *Milton* ends: poised on the verge of the final return to Eternity. If we have been attentive readers, our minds are expanded to the bursting point; and, with our "faculties rouzed to act," we may take the next step into Eternity on our own.

CHAPTER 11

Jerusalem

I *Chapter One*

BLAKE'S *Jerusalem* (c. 1820) recounts the passage of the human consciousness from what we call life ("Eternal Death" to Blake) to authentic life in Eternity. Blake himself writes with "Enthusiasm," accepting the inspiration of Jesus, the human Imagination: "I see the Saviour over me/ Spreading his beams of love & dictating the words of this mild song" (K 622). "Mild" may seem the wrong word for an epic poem filled with anguished incident, but it is right for Blake since his vision will transcend this world of chaos and war to restore us to Eternity.[1]

Unlike Blake, however, Albion at the poem's beginning turns from the Jesus who assures him that "I am not a God afar off . . . Within your bosoms I reside, and you reside in me. . . ." Albion, showing fully the mental habits of one controlled by Urizen, rejects Jerusalem, the imaginative realm that he should inhabit, to say "By demonstration man alone can live" and plans to "build . . . Laws of Moral Virtue" in opposition to "The Spirit of Jesus" which is "continual forgiveness of Sin." Thus Albion is like Urizen "in jealous fears . . . darkening, cold"; and the world that could be humanized is frozen into the alien shapes of the world that we inhabit: ". . . every Human perfection/ Of mountain & river & city are small & wither'd & darken'd."

Blake labors in this poem to resurrect this world to its true humanity which is to be accomplished in the restoration of Jerusalem to Albion. To accomplish this resurrection, he needs ". . . to open the immortal eyes/ Of Man inwards into the Worlds of Thought, into Eternity/ Ever expanding in the Bosom of God, the Human Imagination" (K 623). What he finds at present is that:

... all within is open'd into the deeps of Entuthon Benython,
A dark and unknown night, indefinite, unmeasurable, without end,
Abstract Philosophy warring in enmity against Imagination
(Which is the Divine Body of the Lord Jesus, blessed for ever). . . . (K 624)

The forces at enmity with Imagination are represented in our
fallen world by men like those Blake here names: Hand (probably
Robert Hunt, who wrote the review condemning Blake as an insane
artist), Hyle (probably Hayley, Blake's insensitive "patron"),
Scofield (the soldier Scolfield, who accused Blake of sedition), and
by nine other men. As counterparts, they have twelve female forms
"united into Tirzah" and "in Rahab" as the deceptive natural world
and as the natural theology to which fallen men are drawn. But the
worst enemy of all to the Imagination is within Blake himself, within
the Los side of his personality. That enemy is, of course, the Spectre
of Urthona, all that restrains the imaginative artist in his enthusiasm.

The emanations of the sons of Albion, who are in aggregate the
natural world that we inhabit, offer us the "starry wheels" of the
Newtonian universe. It is the sight of these that strikes terror into the
heart of every imaginative man: thus, for Los, "his Spectre . . .
divided/ In terror of those starry wheels." The Spectre tries to turn
Los against Albion "by tears, by arguments of science & by terrors"
— by the doubts that we all have that cause us to turn away from
Jesus to attend to the terrible starry wheels themselves. The Spectre
can point to all the scorn with which the sons of Albion greet the
products of the Imagination. In addition, he can recount the basic
Blakean story of the fall — the restriction of energy within the fallen
natural world that is carried out with the approval of Urizen and that
ends in "a Law of Sin" such as that by which "Scofield, . . . Kox,
Kotop, and Bowen," participants in Blake's trial in Chichester, tried
to punish him.

Los calmly hears the Spectre's arguments. He asserts his continuing friendship to Albion and forgives enemies of the Imagination:
"O point of mutual forgiveness between Enemies!/ Birthplace of the
Lamb of God incomprehensible" (K 626). Since even Hand (Hunt)
can be overcome, the Spectre poses no real threat ("As thou art now,
such was he, O Spectre."), and Los begins the restoration of Albion.

Los first asserts his control of the furnaces that represent the
dominance of the "physical" over the energetic, the furnaces in
which Luvah is sealed by Vala: "Los [is] the sole, uncontroll'd Lord
of the Furnaces." Since the Imagination ultimately is the origin of

the physical world, art can free the physical world from its false restrictions. Thus, with the "furnaces" open to him, Los can undo the work of the sons of Albion, "for the mighty Hand/ Condens'd his Emanations into hard opake substances,/ And his infant thoughts & desires into cold dark cliffs of death" (K 628). Because of the action of "Hand," the conflict of ideas which should be the intellectual war of Eternity has become the military warfare that surrounds us.

But Los will "form the spiritual sword/ That lays open the hidden heart" to restore "Enthusiasm and Life"; and imaginative art will once again be born from the physical world. To the Spectre, such art is made up of "the Sins/ That thou callest thy Children"; and Los's emanation Enitharmon, the sum total of all his works of art, is the "Great Sin." The Spectre has this view of art because his God "is not a Being of Pity and Compassion,/ He cannot feel Distress, he feeds on Sacrifice & Offering." Los, however, realizes that his Spectre makes "Holy" the "Reasoning Power, And in its Holiness is closed the Abomination of Desolation." He does not see his artistic creations, the Sons of Los, as sins; instead, he calls them from the furnaces to aid in the restoration of Albion's emanation, Jerusalem.

Los and the sons of Los labor to turn London into Golgonooza, the city of art that will properly house Jerusalem and so restore her to Albion. Opposed to their activity is that of the Sons of Albion, who are often represented as a group by Hand, who are trying to build Babylon, the home of Vala. The Sons of Los know that Vala should not be embodied since such an embodiment creates "nature" and natural religion; but the Sons of Albion have already granted Vala her independent existence by permitting the separation of their emanations, Tirzah and Rahab, who together are Vala.

Golgonooza (probably "New Golgotha") will have four gates; and at the center are Luban, Los's palace, and the golden looms of Cathedron, where Jerusalem's web of life is woven.[2] A city built "fourfold" in the wisdom of fully imaginative vision, it lets us see that "the Vegetative Universe opens like a flower from the Earth's center/ In which is Eternity." This city is for Albion what each man's consciousness is for him:

> In those Churches ever consuming & ever building by the Spectres
> Of all the inhabitants of Earth wailing to be Created,
> Shadowy to those who dwell not in them, meer possibilities,
> But to those who enter into them they seem the only substances;

For every thing exists & not one sigh nor smile nor tear,
One hair nor particle of dust, not one can pass away. (K 634)

Golgonooza is that center of reality and truth that no sane man
would deny, except for Locke and Newton: "I turn my eyes to the
Schools & Universities of Europe/ And there behold the Loom of
Locke, whose Woof rages dire,/ Wash'd by the Water-wheels of
Newton . . ." (K 636). Thus Golgonooza contains all of England, as
Blake is at some pains to show us, and all that men have done or felt:

All things acted on Earth are seen in the bright Sculptures of
Los's Halls, & every Age renews its powers from these Works
With every pathetic story possible to happen from Hate or
Wayward Love; & every sorrow & distress is carved here,
Every Affinity of Parents, Marriages & Friendships are here
In all their various combinations wrought with wondrous Art,
All that can happen to Man in his pilgrimage of seventy years.
Such is the Divine Written Law of Horeb & Sinai,
And such the Holy Gospel of Mount Olivet & Calvary. (K 638)

Despite Los's ability to perform the artistic function, he is himself
a victim of the imbalance in the faculties of Albion. Thus, no matter
what he does to stop it, his emanation Enitharmon separates from
him. Even for the visionary artist there is the mundane existence in
which the delusions of space and time are operative. At least Los
knows that Enitharmon (space) *is* his emanation, "Piteous image of
my soft desires & loves"; and he will seek reunion with her.

Meanwhile, the Sons of Albion see Jerusalem as "a sin and
shame" and seek to enthrone Vala in Babylon. In doing this, they
turn on the Imagination and thereby threaten "to destroy the Divine
Saviour." Jerusalem and Vala quarrel in Lambeth, symbolically the
seat of the Church of England, over their respective theological positions. Jerusalem is for Imagination and the forgiveness of sins
("What is Sin but a little/ Error & fault that is soon forgotten?");
Vala is for natural theology and the accusation of sin. And, unfor-
tunately, the deluded Albion intrudes to agree with Vala, sees sin in
Jerusalem, and rejects her. His decision brings about state religion,
whose result is war: " 'Why should Punishment Weave the Veil with
Iron Wheels of War/ When Forgiveness might it Weave with Wings
of Cherubim?' " Thus he joins his sons in a crime against Jesus: " 'O
Human Imagination, O Divine Body I have Crucified,/ I have
turned my back upon thee into the Wastes of Moral Law' " (K 647).

Once, Blake tells us, England was the home of Jerusalem, and its real faith spread over the world: " 'In the Exchanges of Jerusalem every Nation walk'd,/ And London walk'd in every Nation, mutual in love & harmony.' " But now the Sons of Albion build Babylon instead. Only the imaginative remnant that longs for salvation from this world of "Oaken Groves" and "Dragon Temples" pleads: " 'Descend, O Lamb of God, & take away the imputation of Sin/ By the Creation of States & the deliverance of Individuals Evermore. Amen' " (K 648). The destruction of moral categories by forgiveness — forgiveness that "breaks" the Ten Commandments — will remove Vala from Lambeth and allow Golgonooza to replace Babylon. "States" are real categories, but no individual need remain in a state to be punished for a sin.

II *Chapter Two*

Perhaps the most startling assertion made in the latter part of Chapter One of *Jerusalem*, at least for a reader new to Blake, is that Jerusalem was once in England. Blake resumes this argument again in his epistle "To the Jews" that opens Chapter Two. As he asserts, the "inhabitants of Earth" are "united" "in One Religion, The Religion of Jesus." Hence all that surrounds us, whether "England" or "Israel," should be viewed as the emanation of the divine Imagination in us and therefore as Jerusalem. Thus, in the healthy mind, "In the Exchanges of London every Nation walk'd,/ And London walk'd in every Nation." Consequently, it is fair to say that the Jewish patriarchs were "Druids" and that "All things Begin & End in Albion's Ancient Druid Rocky Shore."

After the prose argument, Blake offers all the proof the Imagination would need in a lovely companion lyric to that which begins *Milton:*

> The fields from Islington to Marybone,
> To Primrose Hill and Saint John's Wood,
> Were builded over with pillars of gold,
> And there Jerusalem's pillars stood.

To restore Jerusalem to England, the forgiveness of sins must again dominate British Christianity:

> Forgiving trespasses and sins
> Lest Babylon with cruel Og

> With Moral & Self-righteous Law
> Should Crucify in Satan's Synagogue! (K 650)

At present, however, Albion is so enslaved by moral virtue that, as Chapter Two opens, he sits at Tyburn where the gallows stood and where would now be the "deadly tree" of "Moral Virtue and the Law of God who dwells in Chaos hidden from the human sight." But Jesus, the Divine Vision, again appears behind Kensington Gardens "where was mild Zion Hill's/ Most ancient promontory." Jesus sees the decay in religion that the Sons of Albion have wrought; for Lambeth,[3] seat of the church, London, and Oxford are victims of natural theology: "The City of the Woods in the Forest of Ephratah is taken!/ London is a stone of her ruins, Oxford is the dust of her walls . . ." (K 653).

Since *Jerusalem* began *in medias res*, an account of how Albion fell is useful at this point. This narrative is provided by Enitharmon and the Spectre of Urthona who "alone . . . escaped" from Albion's fall. We are told that Albion created a Urizenic god "from his wearied intellect" and fell to worship it; and this occurrence is, of course, exactly what has befallen the churches in the grip of natural religion (as the speech of Jesus told us). As a result, the "vast form of Nature like a serpent" denies Luvah and Vala their proper roles, and "All is confusion" (K 655).

Los holds the escaped Enitharmon and Spectre of Urthona, aspects of fallen art, within him; and he tours the ruins of Jerusalem in London and finally rests on London Stone near Tyburn. He hears the contentions of Jerusalem and Vala: Jerusalem argues for "Faith" against "Demonstration," and Vala maintains that "Urizen is the Champion of Albion." All events seem to support Vala's cause. The Sons of Albion build "Druid . . . Temples," and Albion's Rational Power ("the Great Selfhood,/ Satan, Worship'd as God by the Mighty Ones of the Earth") appears to denounce everything that is human. Vala follows up to assert that, in any case, the human form is just another natural form and not a spiritual one ("The Imaginative Human Form is but a breathing of Vala"). In her, the female will (natural law) triumphs:

> . . . what may Woman be
> To have power over Man from Cradle to corruptible Grave?
> There is a Throne in every Man, it is the Throne of God;
> This, Woman has claim'd as her own, & Man is no more! (K 661)

The Divine Humanity has already been denied in Vala's previous assertion that she creates even the human form. From Blake's time forward, "scientific" accounts of man have been based on the assumptions of the total materialism that she represents.

"Reuben" enters the myth at this point to represent man fallen to the level that Vala has defined. He is a natural man or, as Blake puts it, "vegetative man"; but "Merlin," who is also present, suggests the possibility of a still imaginative man. Fortunately, man will fall no lower than Reuben (a sort of Adam) because Jesus has set "the two limits, Satan and Adam," the limits of opacity and contraction; therefore, we will not see a world more stonified than we now see, nor will we see man as less than Reuben or Adam. When the Divine Imagination sets these limits, the act is essentially the same as that of Los who fixed the changes of Urizen; but here the imaginative act is seen from its positive side as an act of mercy.

Our world perceived as "Elements" and as "Length, Bredth & Highth" is formed as it was in *The Book of Urizen*. The Eternals find our moral laws absurd:

> "Have you known the Judgment that is arisen among the
> Zoas of Albion, where a Man dare hardly to embrace
> His own Wife for the terrors of Chastity that they call
> By the name of Morality?" (K 663)

But Albion keeps his humanity bound in "petrific hardness" and keeps away all that might touch "His hidden heart." Jesus follows him to offer the hope of Vision, while London urges him "let us awake up together," but Albion is unmoved; he is looking for "Atonement," which the law would demand, rather than for mercy. Los points, without effect upon Albion, to the cruel vision of spiritual existence to which Albion chooses to adhere: " 'Must the Wise die for an Atonement? does Mercy endure Atonement?/ No! It is Moral Severity & destroys Mercy in its Victim' " (K 666). All England mourns Albion's mistaken theology, saying "he hath studied the arts/ Of unbelief" (K 667). The cathedral cities of England, the possessors of "A Human Vision! Human Divine, Jesus the Saviour, blessed for ever and ever," yearn for Albion's restoration.

Albion curses his "own affections/ And his own beloveds," the potentially visionary aspects of himself that he beholds in Los's furnaces — even within art that must use a fallen world and that demands "righteousness & justice." But Los refuses to let Albion destroy "these little ones," his emotions; and he asserts that he himself can, as a visionary, "break [Albion's] bonds of righteousness." Los also indicates that, although man can fall no lower than Adam and nature, he can, when his imagination is freed, expand to infinity: ". . . there is no Limit of Expansion; there is no Limit of Translucence/ In the bosom of Man for ever from eternity to eternity." Los knows that we need only call on "ourselves, in whom God dwells," to find the "Divine Humanity" again. He seeks support from the cathedral cities in particular, asking that they counter the natural religion that builds Druid temples "instead of heavenly Chapels built/ By our dear Lord."

Only Bath of the cathedral cities responds to Los's plea by saying that "none but the Lamb of God can heal/ This dread disease, none but Jesus." Bath gets Oxford to "take . . . the leaves of the Tree of Life" (probably the Bible, printed in Oxford[4]); and Oxford asks Albion to stay with the cathedral cities until his perceptual and theological error can be removed: " '. . . Repose upon our bosoms/ Till the plow of Jehovah and the Harrow of Shaddai/ Have passed over the Dead to awake the Dead to Judgment' " (K 676). Albion, who has lost all other hope (K 677), submits and sinks into the arms of Jesus. He is put to sleep on a couch with sixteen pillars that are made of the books of the Bible that Blake most admires.[5] Now Erin, the spirit of Ireland, is able to rise to speak about the errors of perception and thought that have led to Albion's plight:

"The Visions of Eternity, by reason of narrowed perceptions,
Are become weak Visions of Time & Space, fix'd into furrows of death,
. . . .
Withering the Human Form by Laws of Sacrifice for Sin." (K 679)

She announces the possibility of forgiveness of sins, for men fall into mistaken states of mind and perception. These mental states cannot be "forgiven" since they *are* errors, but individuals can be forgiven for their having entered such states. Therefore, she prays for the coming of Jesus with forgiveness of sins; and the Daughters of Beulah, carriers of artistic inspiration to a fallen world, respond: "Come then, O Lamb of God, and take away the remembrance of Sin" (K 681). And Chapter Two ends with Albion asleep on the bosom of the cathedral cities, and the coming of Jesus is awaited so that Albion can be restored.

III *Chapter Three*

The third chapter of *Jerusalem* depicts the triumph of natural religion and natural morality and of the epistemology on which they are based. Accordingly, Blake's prefatory epistle, this time addressed "To the Deists," asserts that "He never can be a Friend to the Human Race who is the Preacher of Natural Morality or Natural Religion." Because Satan is the Accuser of Sin, "Every Religion that Preaches Vengeance for Sin is the Religion of the Enemy & Avenger and not of the Forgiver of Sin. . . ." Against the natural religionists, Blake identifies himself ("We") with "the Spiritually Religious" whether "a Monk, or a Methodist." He also defends Whitefield and, as expected, denounces Voltaire and Rousseau. Warfare is never caused by "poor Monks & Religious," he concludes, but by the natural religionists, a point that Chapter Three demonstrates.

In the lyric that follows and picks up these themes, Blake depicts a monk's suffering under a warlike state and moves to a defense of the emotions, "the little ones," that Albion rejected in Chapter Two:

> Titus! Constantine! Charlemaine!
> O Voltaire! Rousseau! Gibbon! Vain
> Your Grecian Mocks & Roman Sword
> Against this image of his Lord!
>
> For a Tear is an Intellectual thing,
> And a Sigh is the Sword of an Angel King,
> And the bitter groan of a Martyr's woe
> Is an Arrow from the Almightie's Bow. (K 683)

"Fear and Hope are — Vision" (K 768), Blake wrote; and every Monk and Methodist knows that visionary truth resides in emotion, despite the natural religionists and despite Albion's present fallen condition.

Albion's rational power tells him that the "Friend of Sinners" is a "Rebel against my Laws"; he is ready to accept whatever the daughters of Albion, the separated emanation of the sons of Albion and the representatives of delusive nature, tell him. Los, however, labors on; he is building Golgonooza with the assistance of the Eternals who always exist within the Imagination to counteract the "generalizing Demonstrations of the Rational Power." The Daughters of Albion repeat Vala's assertion of the "female" power of nature over man:

". . . what may Woman be
To have power over Man from Cradle to corruptible Grave?
He who is an Infant and whose Cradle is a Manger
Knoweth the Infant sorrow, whence it came and where it goeth
And who weave it a Cradle of the grass that withereth away.
This World is all a Cradle for the erred wandering Phantom,
Rock'd by Year, Month, Day & Hour; and every two Moments
Between dwells a Daughter of Beulah to feed the Human Vegetable."

(K 688)

Only in the sustaining visits of inspiration between "two moments"
by a Daughter of Beulah does man's real nutriment arrive. All that is
subject to the Daughters of Albion, to "nature," is "the human
Vegetable." But, arrogantly, the Daughters choose to misunder-
stand the Incarnation as proof that all is subject to nature.

Bath, Canterbury, York, and Edinburgh, the cathedral cities, join
Los in his opposition to the Daughters of Albion to no avail. Jesus
tries in vain to summon back Jerusalem, who is ".clos'd in the
Dungeons of Babylon"; but only Los seems to hear Jesus say, "I am
the Resurrection & the Life" and thus "live[s] and breathe[s] in
hope"; for the intellectual side of man, represented by the sons of
Urizen, is given over to the arts of war:

Then left the Sons of Urizen the plow & harrow, the loom,
The hammer & the chisel & the rule & compasses; from London fleeing,
They forg'd the sword on Cheviot, the chariot of war & the battle-ax. . . .

(K 699)

They are fully the victims of a faulty epistemology: "In ignorance to
view a small portion & think that All,/ And call it Demonstration,
blind to all the simple rules of life" (K 700).

For the sons of Albion, the result of such thought is war — not the
intellectual wars of Eternity but those carried on in behalf of
jealousy and moral virtue:

"Is not the wound of the sword sweet & the broken bone delightful?
Wilt thou now smile among the scythes when the wounded groan in the
    field?
We were carried away in thousands from London & in tens
Of thousands from Westminster & Marybone, in ships clos'd up,
Chain'd hand & foot, compell'd to fight under the iron whips
Of our captains, fearing our officers more than the enemy." (K 700)

And the sons of both Urizen and Albion contribute to the building of Stonehenge, the triumph of natural religion, where the sacrifice of children and the punishment of "sinners" can be carried out. One passage descriptive of Stonehenge summarizes much of Blake's thought about the triumph of natural religion:

> The Building is Natural Religion & its Altars Natural Morality,
> A building of eternal death, whose proportions are eternal despair.
> Here Vala stood turning the iron Spindle of destruction
> From heaven to earth, howling, invisible; but not invisible,
> Her Two Covering Cherubs, afterwards named Voltaire & Rousseau,
> Two frowning Rocks on each side of the Cove & Stone of Torture,
> Frozen Sons of the feminine Tabernacle of Bacon, Newton & Locke;
> For Luvah is France, the Victim of the Spectres of Albion. (K 702)

The worship of feminine "nature" has resulted from the empiricism of "Bacon, Newton & Locke." And its result has been war on France that is to Blake an effect of state religion, a secularized religion, dominated by natural morality, that interests itself in statecraft.

Under the tyranny of natural religion, men's senses are made to shrink; and the universe becomes even more alien:

> The Stars flee remote; the heaven is iron, the earth is sulphur,
> And all the mountains & hills shrink up like a withering gourd
> As the Senses of Men shrink together under the Knife of flint
> In the hands of Albion's Daughters among the Druid Temples. (K 703)

Now the Daughters of Albion can be seen as Tirzah (the natural world) and Rahab (corrupt, institutionalized religion). Together they preach materialism: "Calling the Rocks Atomic Origins of Existence, denying Eternity/ By the Atheistical Epicurean Philosophy of Albion's Tree" (K 704). They bring about the condemnation of Jerusalem, particularly the Liberty that she represents: "Drawing the free loves of Jerusalem into infernal bondage/ That they might be born in contentions of Chastity & in Deadly Hate . . ." (K 707).

The sex act is for most fallen men their one imaginative act; therefore, since sex is their only insight into Jerusalem, this act must particularly be denounced by natural religion because it fears any outbreak of the imaginative. Such an attitude, as we have seen before (". . . Brothels [are built] with bricks of Religion"), creates "A Religion of Chastity, forming a Commerce to sell Loves."

Hand has by now become a horrible analytic monster:

His bosom wide & shoulders huge, overspreading wondrous,
Bear Three strong sinewy Necks & Three awful & terrible Heads,
Three Brains, in contradictory council brooding incessantly,
Neither daring to put in act its councils, fearing each-other,
Therefore rejecting Ideas as nothing & holding all Wisdom
To consist in the agreements & disagreements of Ideas,
Plotting to devour Albion's Body of Humanity & Love. (K 708)

Within the monster, representing "Bacon & Newton & Locke" as
well as Hand, Rahab sits "Imputing Sin & Righteousness to Individuals" and creating "Abstract Philosophy to destroy Imagination, the Divine Humanity." And Rahab is in turn identified as Vala
(K 709).

All the geography of the British Isles is, of course, a map of the
fallen Albion. In Eternity, all is human:

For all are Men in Eternity, Rivers, Mountains, Cities, Villages,
All are Human, & when you enter into their Bosoms you walk
In Heavens & Earths, as in your own Bosom you bear your Heaven
And Earth & all you behold; tho' it appears Without, it is Within,
In your Imagination, of Which this World of Mortality is but a Shadow.
(K 709)

And thus Blake devotes two plates (71 and 72) to outlining which
parts of England, Scotland, Wales, and Ireland belong to each of the
sons and daughters of Albion. And, since Jerusalem will overspread
all nations, he lists the nations but combines them to reduce their
number to thirty-two. Missing from these lists, however, is
Golgonooza, which still belongs to Los. Blake describes one of the
gates of the New Jerusalem:

Fenelon, Guion, Teresa,
Whitefield & Hervey guard that Gate, with all the gentle Souls
Who guide the great Wine-press of Love. Four precious Stones that Gate.
(K 712)

Those who understand the role of emotion, who murder not the "little ones," include the three great mystics (Fenelon, Guyon, Theresa
of Avila), the "Methodist" Whitefield, and the Evangelical Anglican
Hervey; and they have a special role to play in showing us the way
back to the heavenly city.

Los struggles at his anvil to undo the works of Deists like Voltaire,
who would consider the limit of Opacity and the limit of Contraction

not as the boundaries of our mental error but as proof of God's cruelty to mankind:

> Voltaire insinuates that these Limits are the cruel work of God,
> Mocking the Remover of Limits & the Resurrection of the Dead,
> Setting up Kings in wrath, in holiness of Natural Religion:
> Which Los with his mighty Hammer demolishes time on time
> In miracles & wonders in the Four-fold Desart of Albion. (K 713)

God removes limits and resurrects men; he doesn't impose limitation, and this freedom the visionary artist can prove. Blake prays for the full inspiration Los has:

> Teach me, O Holy Spirit, the Testimony of Jesus! let me
> Comprehend wonderous things out of the Divine Law!
> I behold Babylon in the opening Streets of London. I behold
> Jerusalem in ruins wandering about from house to house. (K 714)

He sees how bad theology and bad epistemology have brought bad art: "Harmonies of Concords & Discords/ Opposed to Melody, and by Lights & Shades opposed to Outline,/ And by Abstractions opposed to the Visions of Imagination" (K 715). And also he sees how natural religion has brought sexual repression and war:

> Babylon, the Rational Morality, deluding to death the little ones
> In strong temptations of stolen beauty. I tell how Reuben slept
> On London Stone, & the Daughters of Albion ran around admiring
> His awful beauty; with Moral Virtue, the fair deciever, offspring
> Of Good & Evil, they divided him in love upon the Thames & sent
> Him over Europe, in streams of gore. . . . (K 715)

Reuben, the natural man and now the complete victim, passes into the bloody conflicts of Europe "in streams of gore."

All the centuries of false religion stand revealed to Blake from "Adam to Luther" and on through the natural religion of Rahab. But still Blake's vision can center on "Jesus, breaking thro' the Central Zones of Death & Hell, [who]/ Opens Eternity in Time & Space, triumphant in Mercy" (K 716). Albion is fully fallen into the delusions of empiricism ("the starry Heavens are fled from the mighty limbs of Albion"), into the cruelties of natural morality, and into natural theology. But the prophets, Los and Blake, are ready to begin his restoration.

IV   *Chapter Four*

The concluding chapter of *Jerusalem* is addressed to the Christians. The errors of the Deists have now solidified and become dominant in "Christian" England. Now, in Blake's own time, the Christians have reached a dead end that they can escape only by exercising the "Divine Arts of Imagination" rather than rationality and the systems of natural religion. Blake admits to the Satanic wheels that have come to dominate our perception:

> I stood among my valleys of the south
> And saw a flame of fire, even as a Wheel
> Of fire surrounding all the heavens: it went
> From west to east, against the current of
> Creation, and devour'd all things in its loud
> Fury & thundering course round heaven & earth.
> By it the Sun was roll'd into an orb,
> By it the Moon faded into a globe
> Travelling thro' the night. . . . (K 717)

Such wheels are not only physical but also moral systems: "Is this the law of Jesus,/ This terrible devouring sword turning every way?" Fortunately, the answer to Blake's question is no; what he sees is only the wheel of mistaken natural religion, while in truth "Jesus is the bright Preacher of Life/ Creating Nature from this fiery Law/ By self-denial & forgiveness of Sin" (K 718). "Creating Nature" in Blake's sense is un-creating the delusive nature that we see so that Eternity can be restored. This process of renewal is carried out not by application of the law but through "forgiveness" which destroys all systems of law. Blake ends his preface with another lyric that appeals for the restoration of Jerusalem to England.

Rahab, institutionalized natural religion, is seen as enthroned at the outset of Chapter Four with "power over the earth." Jerusalem is an outcast: " 'How distant far from Albion! his hills & valleys no more/ Receive the feet of Jerusalem: they have cast me quite away,/ And Albion is himself shrunk to a narrow rock in the midst of the sea!' " (K 720). Vala in her confused state fears that, should Jesus return, He would revive Albion and permit him to slay her Luvah. Hand and Hyle are fully enslaved by their feminine emanations, Cambel and Gwendolen, who are separated objects of perception and who are therefore able to tyrannize over the perceiver as does the empiricist's world. Cambel and Gwendolen congratulate themselves on having driven away Merlin, the imaginative man; but they still fear that they will "perish annihilate" if they do not carry out their binding and limiting of the human mind with sufficient thoroughness.

Thus, on the surface, the situation seems little changed from Chapter Three; but what is significantly different is the increasing note of desperation among the forces of evil. As Blake says, "he who will not bend to Love must be subdued by Fear." Natural religion proves inadequate to man's needs, and rationality leads to the despair about reason's power and about human nature that the eighteenth century saw in David Hume. Error has taken definite shape, and it will make destruction all the easier to carry out.

Los is still dedicated to his vision, and has an ever-increasing sense of his powers and his role. The solidification of error and error's growing lack of confidence in itself will make his task easier to accomplish. Los can say, "I know I am Urthona, keeper of the Gates of Heaven/ And that I can at will expatiate in the Gardens of bliss." He knows that daughters of Albion, like those worshipped by Hand and Hyle, weave only "An outside shadowy Surface superadded to the real Surface/ Which is unchangeable for ever & ever."

And Albion's daughters have a growing sense of loss, like that which characterized the work of Lord Byron, a knowledge of a lost paradise from which their rationality now bars them: "Our Father Albion's land, O it was a lovely land!" Once, as emanations of healthy sons of Albion, " 'We builded Jerusalem as a City & a Temple; from Lambeth/ We began our Foundations, lovely Lambeth' " (K 729). They know that they are really enslaved now (even though they are in turn the enslavers of Albion) because they are compelled to "build Babylon on Euphrates" in the service of mistaken notions of perception. They see what their labors have cost British civilization: "I see London, blind & age-bent, begging thro' the Streets/ Of Babylon, led by a child" (K 729). They now fear even their victim Hand, who "combines into a Mighty-one, the Double Molech & Chemosh," the gods of sacrifice and war.

Los offers a Song in praise of his constant vision of Jerusalem within Albion:

"I see thy Form, O lovely mild Jerusalem, wing'd with Six Wings
In the opacous Bosom of the Sleeper, lovely Three-fold
In Head & Heart & Reins, three Universes of love & beauty.
Thy forehead bright, Holiness to the Lord, with Gates of pearl

Reflects Eternity; beneath, thy azure wings of feathery down
Ribb'd delicate & cloth'd with feather'd gold & azure & purple,
From thy white shoulders shadowing purity in holiness!" (K 730–31)

Los's artistic vision has achieved such clarity of outline that Eternity
cannot be far off; but a last-ditch counter-world, based on a false
definition of man, has also been under construction. The Daughters
of Albion started it by building "a Space & an Allegory around the
Winding Worm" that Hyle has become. This world is one that is institutionalized rather than spontaneous; it is "an Earthly Kingdom"
where the Daughters of Albion "reign in pride & to oppress & to mix
the Cup of Delusion." What they create is State Religion —
religious insight that was forced into the framework of the state, as
was to be found in Rome, or that materialized in England under the
Puritans. (The seeds of the spiritual kingdom must constantly be
planted by the Daughters of Beulah, by inspiration.) Los mistakenly
brings Reuben (natural man) into this kingdom because of his artist's
wish to make Enitharmon ("space") actually embody the ideal. But,
since contact with institutions based on materialistic assumptions is
always destructive of the spiritual, the result of this attempt is a
repetition of the separation of Enitharmon from Los and finally the
appearance of the Covering Cherub, the Anti-Christ of State
Religion:

. . . in selfish holiness:
The Pharisaion, the Grammateis, the Presbuterion,
The Archiereus, the Iereus, the Saddusaion: double
Each withoutside of the other, covering eastern heaven.
Thus was the Covering Cherub reveal'd, majestic image
Of Selfhood, Body put off, the Antichrist accursed,
Cover'd with precious stones: a Human Dragon terrible
And bright stretch'd over Europe & Asia gorgeous.
In three nights he devour'd the rejected corse of death.
His Head, dark, deadly, in its Brain incloses a reflexion
Of Eden all perverted. . . . (K 734)

Jerusalem is "Hidden within the Covering Cherub"; and Los,
whatever his mistakes before, knows that this institutionalized error
must be overcome:

    "Go to these fiends of Righteousness,
Tell them to obey their Humanities & not pretend Holiness
When they are murderers: as far as my Hammer & Anvil permit.

Go, tell them that the Worship of God is honouring his gifts
In other men: & loving the greatest men best, each according
To his Genius: which is the Holy Ghost in Man; there is no other
God than that God who is the intellectual fountain of Humanity.
He who envies or calumniates, which is murder & cruelty,
Murders the Holy-one. Go, tell them this, & overthrow their cup,
Their bread, their altar-table, their incense & their oath,
Their marriage & their baptism, their burial & consecration.
I have tried to make friends by corporeal gifts but have only
Made enemies. I never made friends but by spiritual gifts,
By severe contentions of friendship & the burning fire of thought.
He who would see the Divinity must see him in his Children,
One first, in friendship & love, then a Divine Family, & in the midst
Jesus will appear; so he who wishes to see a Vision, a perfect Whole,
Must see it in its Minute Particulars, Organized, & not as thou,
O Fiend of Righteousness, pretendest; thine is a Disorganized
And snowy cloud, brooder of tempests & destructive War.
You smile with pomp & rigor, you talk of benevolence & virtue;
I act with benevolence & Virtue & get murder'd time after time.
You accumulate Particulars & murder by analyzing, that you
May take the aggregate, & you call the aggregate Moral Law,
And you call that swell'd & bloated Form a Minute Particular;
But General Forms have their vitality in Particulars, & every
Particular is a Man, a Divine Member of the Divine Jesus." (K 738)

The institution and rites of the church have been worshipped far more than the God in every man. Enitharmon, the projection of Los as the institutionalized church is the projection of the winding worm, fears that she will "annihilate vanish for ever" (K 739). And, in a sense, she must because, as Los says, "Sexes must vanish & cease/ To be when Albion arises from his dread repose . . ." (K 739). But the vanishing of sexes means simply that, in the case of Enitharmon, she will return to the breast of Los, her source, even as "the Church," properly understood, will return to the heart of man.

Los now sees the coming of the Anti-Christ, the solidification of error, as the promised signal for the apocalypse:

"Fear not, my Sons, this waking Death; he is become One with me.
Behold him here! We shall not Die! we shall be united in Jesus.
Will you suffer this Satan, this Body of Doubt that Seems but Is Not,
To occupy the very threshold of Eternal Life? if Bacon, Newton, Locke
Deny a Conscience in Man & the Communion of Saints & Angels,
Contemning the Divine Vision & Fruition, Worshiping the Deus,
Of the Heathen, the God of This World, & the Goddess Nature,

Mystery, Babylon the Great, The Druid Dragon & hidden Harlot,
Is it not that Signal of the Morning which was told us in the Beginning?"
                                                              (K 741)

And, indeed,

Time was Finished! The Breath Divine Breathed over Albion
Beneath the Furnaces & starry Wheels and in the Immortal Tomb,
And England, who is Brittannia, awoke from Death on Albion's bosom:
She awoke pale & cold; she fainted seven times on the Body of Albion.
"O pitious Sleep, O pitious Dream! O God, O God awake! I have slain
In Dreams of Chastity & Moral Law: I have Murdered Albion! Ah!
In Stone-henge & on London Stone & in the Oak Groves of Malden
I have slain him in my Sleep with the Knife of the Druid. O England!
O all ye Nations of the Earth, behold ye the Jealous Wife!
The Eagle & the Wolf & Monkey & Owl & the King & Priest were there."
                                                              (K 742)

England returns to Albion's breast, putting an end to the concept of
a "state" that is external to us and makes laws for us. Jesus appears:

. . . standing by Albion as the Good Shepherd
By the lost Sheep that he hath found, & Albion knew that it
Was the Lord, the Universal Humanity; & Albion saw his Form
A Man, & they conversed as Man with Man in Ages of Eternity.
And the Divine Appearance was the likeness & similitude of Los. (K 743)

Jesus must resemble Los because both are the Imagination. Jesus
calls Los to self-sacrifice, brotherhood, and the forgiveness of sins.
Albion picks up the "Bow of Mercy and Loving-kindness" and the
"Arrows of Love" and with them slays the "Druid spectre" of law
and punishment. "Milton & Shakspear & Chaucer," imaginative
men, appear in heaven as "Chariots of the Almighty"; but so do
"Bacon & Newton & Locke" since all men's faculties are now in-
dicative of divinity.
     The mind of man is free to create:

And they conversed together in Visionary forms dramatic which bright
Redounded from their Tongues in thunderous majesty, in Visions
In new Expanses, creating exemplars of Memory and of Intellect,
Creating Space, Creating Time, according to the wonders Divine
Of Human Imagination. . . . (K 746)

All false institutions and systems are gone (K 746); the world is at last seen for what it is, a product of the Imagination: "All Human Forms identified, even Tree, Metal, Earth & Stone." All these are emanations from us, as is London, and England, and the Universe. In the aggregate, the projections from the Divine Imagination are Jerusalem: "And I heard the Name of their Emanations: they are named Jerusalem" (K 747).

V *The Themes of* Jerusalem

Clearly a specific concern that Blake pursues in *Jerusalem* is the restoration of the English Church which, he argues, must be freed from the secularization seen in its involvement in political matters ("State Religion") and which must be purged of its reliance on reason rather than on vision. Above all, the Church must renounce the accusation of sin, Satan's province, and adopt the forgiveness of sins to which Jesus summons it. In this respect, Blake's themes in *Jerusalem* may seem "doctrinal," conditioned by his wish to make "Lambeth" the center of a vital faith again. But we must recognize that Blake's usual assumption that "All things Begin & End in Albion's Ancient Druid Rocky Shore" is operative in *Jerusalem*. In seeking the restoration of a healthy theology to England, *Jerusalem* can picture the entire process by which the Imagination is restored, despite the threats and restrictions that it must overcome. Blake's last published work, it offers his message completely and triumphantly. Blake never faltered in the faith that it sets forth.

Conclusion

I   *The Themes of William Blake*

SUCH VISIONS HAVE APPEARED TO ME
AS I MY ORDERED RACE HAVE RUN.
JERUSALEM IS NAMED LIBERTY
AMONG THE SONS OF ALBION.
Jerusalem (K 649)

WILLIAM Blake's primary concern is the restoration to mankind of the clear vision and the perfect freedom of Eternity. He urges that all men share in this "Building up of Jerusalem," and he asks for the creation of an artistic and theological milieu in which "all the Lord's people" can be "Prophets." Some of his works describe how the fall from Eternity occurred and depict the destructive effects on the powers of the human mind which that fall has had. *The Book of Urizen* and *The Four Zoas* effectively recreate this process through their mythic presentation of the warring facilities — reason, imagination, energy, and integrative perception — faculties that must work in unison if we are to regain the genuine Humanity of Eternity. In Eternity, Jesus, the Human Form Divine, ever present but denied by the rational faculty, will exist: "He in us, and we in Him." But, as *Milton* and *Jerusalem* make clear, a theology tied to nature and to moral codes, and one that does not practice the forgiveness of sins, cannot lead us back to our Divine Humanity. Such a theology does not free Humanity but restricts it; it ignores the fact that Jerusalem is "named Liberty" among the sons of Albion.

Blake's definition of genuine liberty requires that we reject the illusion of man's having a place in nature, an error that Blake explores in *The Book of Thel* and in the three fine cyclical poems in the

Pickering Manuscript. We must learn to trust the intuition of the *Songs of Innocence* that humanity belongs to a better world than this one; we must see that the inadequate natural, social, and institutional world of the *Songs of Experience* hovers on the brink of an apocalypse that threatens to erupt when we are bold enough to ask "The Tyger" — or any seemingly inhuman power in the world — why it exists. In our study of Blake's views of nature in these works, we are guided in our responses by Blake's combined arts of poetry and engraving. Every plate exists independently to offer within itself a specific statement on the inadequacy of the views depicted. The works are difficult for the "Corporeal Understanding," but they are meant to speak to the "Intellectual Powers." They deny, therefore, the validity of nature in the very mode by which they speak to us.

In works like *The Marriage of Heaven and Hell, Visions of the Daughters of Albion,* and *The French Revolution* Blake attacks the codes of morality and the systems of law that deny the revolutionary energy in us that could lead us back to Eternity. He advocates "Impulse" and not "Rule," and he denies that we can make laws for others: "One Law for the Lion and the Ox is Oppression." Political revolutions, like those in France and America, are simply proof that the mind of man is expanding toward the freedom of Eternity. Blake thus strongly advocates both sexual and political freedom, but he warns that both are steps on the road to genuine liberty rather than the goals in themselves that Paine or Voltaire would make them. Blake's warning about the limitations of the merely secular is at times ignored by some among the large numbers of readers now drawn to his works.

II *Blake's Growing Influence*

The scholarship of the last fifty years has made Blake sufficiently accessible to serious readers of poetry for us to be quite confident that Blake's influence will now spread. Indeed, any college teacher of literature can attest to a wildfire spread of interest in Blake's work among students. Blake is now in a position to become a significant force in our culture: his influence will be felt in many attempts to find a way out of what it is common to call the "modern predicament"; and it will be felt in the theories of art held by major artists and critics.

The anguished drift toward Nihilism that has characterized the modern temper can be checked and reversed only by a thinker who can show us how to transcend the habits of empiricism and rationality to which our minds have been bound since the work of Bacon, Newton, and Locke. At least three major Romantic poets in England offer to show us the way out: Blake, Wordsworth, and Coleridge; for these writers all take as their subject the mind — its fall into error and its restoration to health through the Imagination. But Blake perhaps succeeds best of these three by striking through the veil of error with the simple — not metaphorical but quite literal — statement that the Imagination is Jesus. On the basis of this assertion, Blake's impressively coherent vision can offer a new morality and a new politics based on the eradication of all that restrains the Imagination. Blake points toward the "post-modern" world more confidently and more convincingly than any other Romantic thinker.[1]

One element in Blake that astonishes the modern reader is Blake's confident reliance on a Christian stance in the face of threats to it that neither twentieth-century science nor twentieth-century philosophy can make more damagingly than they were made to Blake's age by men like David Hume. As eccentric a figure as Blake seemed to his readers in the first hundred years after his death, he now seems the one Romantic who most adheres to the defining force of our civilization, Christianity. We can now understand Blake's easy linking of himself with Isaiah and Ezekiel and his contentions with fellow prophets like Dante and Milton. We can now understand what he meant in saying that Wordsworth was not a "Bible Christian." Blake turns out after all to be the one Romantic who fits most comfortably into Judaeo-Christian traditions of thought and art. "Secular" and "humanist" approaches to Blake have had their successes, but Blake's theology will receive serious attention in the future. His special relevance to us all may well be in the fact that he offers to heal the crisis in our civilization by demonstrating that it is threatened with dissolution only because it fails to heed the Saviour who is, literally for Blake, within each man.

Blake's influence on artistic theory should be to further artistic practice and critical theory that is epistemologically informed. When it is recognized that there is significant shape in all perception and that what is perceived is provided by the mental condition of the perceiver, artistic objects will be recognized as projections of states of mind that are meaningful in every detail and that can be described in terms of whether they display imagination that is free or fettered. Northrop Frye, who names Blake as the major influence on his work, has initiated a criticism that attempts to speak of the meaning of literary form in much this way. Thanks to Blake, as well as Frye, critical theory is certain to continue to move in this direction.

Blake is winning a place in a civilization to which he once seemed an utter outsider. If the devotion of the young is any indication, he will help restore and lead that civilization. But he offers us even more — the cleansing of our vision to make possible the reassumption of our Divine Humanity. He is both a major poet and a central one, and he is fully the product of all that is vital in the history of Western thought and art. We now are inclined to listen to him when he offers to show us how to "be happy."

Notes and References

Chapter One

1. The most reliable of the nineteenth-century accounts of Blake's life is Alexander Gilchrist, *Life of William Blake, "Pictor Ignotus"* (London, 1863), two volumes. Other nineteenth-century biographical accounts, all quite brief, are collected in Joseph Anthony Wittreich, Jr., ed., *Nineteenth-Century Accounts of William Blake* (Gainesville, Florida, 1970). For an intelligent evaluation of the work of the nineteenth-century biographers and a skillful compilation of all available facts about Blake, G. E. Bentley, Jr.'s *Blake Records* (Oxford, 1970) should be consulted.

2. For Law's influence on John Wesley, see Eric W. Baker, *A Herald of the Evangelical Revival* (London, 1948).

3. For Law's impact on English Swedenborgians, see, for instance, Theodore Compton, *The Life and Correspondence of the Reverend John Clowes* (London, 1874), pp. 14–15.

4. T. B. Shepherd, *Methodism and the Literature of the Eighteenth Century* (London, 1940), p. 243. Actually, Shepherd's comment is made in response to a similar remark by Gilbert Thomas.

5. W. E. Gladstone, *Correspondence on Church and Religion*, ed. D. C. Lathbury (New York, 1910), I, 7–8.

6. See *Blake Records*, pp. 7–8.

7. See Nancy Bogen, "The Problem of Blake's Early Religion," *The Personalist*, XLIV (1968), 509–22.

8. Gilchrist, I, 7. Blake's childhood visions were by no means unique in England in this period; for a similar event, see *The Life and Correspondence of the Reverend John Clowes*, p. 37.

9. Stanley Gardner, *Blake* (London, 1968), pp. 18–23.

10. This account apparently has its origin in a letter written by Blake. See *Blake Records*, p. 13 and n.

11. Gilchrist, I, 267.

12. *Ibid.*, 35.

13. *Ibid.*, 38.

14. The phrase appears in William Blake, *Selected Writings*, ed. Robert Gleckner (New York, 1967), p. xxiii, and in Kathleen Raine, *William Blake* (New York, 1970), p. 27.

15. Martin K. Nurmi, *William Blake* (London, 1975), p. 35.

16. Samuel C. Chew, "The Nineteenth Century and After," in *A Literary History of England*, ed. Albert C. Baugh (New York, 1948), p. 1130.

17. Many readers find poems like "Holy Thursday" in *Innocence* to be ironic in intention. This approach to the state of Innocence robs it of its visionary power. See Chapter 7.

18. Gilchrist, I, 57.

19. *Ibid.*, 59.

20. *Ibid.*, 68.

21. *Ibid.*, 69.

22. *Blake Records*, p. 36. The words are taken from Professor Bentley's summary of the resolutions passed at the meeting.

23. The signatures have not themselves survived but are transcribed in Swedenborgian records.

24. J. G. Davies, *The Theology of William Blake* (Oxford, 1948), p. 34.

25. Richard Price, "A Discourse on the Love of our Country," in *The Debate on the French Revolution, 1789–1800*, ed. Alfred Cobban (London, 1950), pp. 63–64.

26. Hayley quoted in *Blake Records*, p. 78. Hayley's correspondence in this period abounds in variations on this patronizing formula applied to Blake.

27. *Ibid.*, p. 125.

28. *Ibid.*, p. 215.

29. *Ibid.*, p. 197.

30. Frederick Tatham suggested that Blake's "eccentric speeches were thrown forth more as a piece of sarcasm upon the inquirer than from his real opinion." See Tatham, "The Life of William Blake," in *Nineteenth-Century Accounts of William Blake*, p. 234.

31. From a letter written by George Richmond and published in Gilchrist, I, 362.

32. *Ibid.*, 330.

33. *Ibid.*, 361.

34. From an anonymous account quoted — and defended — in *Blake Records*, pp. 373–74.

Chapter Two

1. For a condensed discussion of this process and its effect on the structure of the "narrative" portion of Blake's artistic product, see David V. Erdman, *The Poetry and Prose of William Blake* (New York, 1965), pp. 712–13.

2. Harold Bloom, "The Visionary Cinema of Romantic Poetry," in *William Blake: Essays for S. Foster Damon*, ed. Alvin H. Rosenfeld (Providence, 1969), p. 22.

3. See Karl Kroeber, "Graphic-Poetic Structuring in Blake's *Book of Urizen*," *Blake Studies*, III (1970), 9: "The 'narrative flow,' so to speak, of the prophecy is constrained . . . by the distinct aesthetic integrity of each engraved plate."

4. Northrop Frye, "The Road of Excess," in *The Stubborn Structure: Essays on Criticism and Society* (London, 1970), p. 164 and p. 162.

5. S. Foster Damon, *William Blake: His Philosophy and Symbols* (Boston, 1924), p. 354.

6. Actually, "the plates cannot be shifted about absolutely arbitrarily." (Kroeber, 13).

7. S. Foster Damon, *A Blake Dictionary* (New York, 1971), p. 419.

8. *Ibid.*, p. 458.

Chapter Three

1. Gardner, p. 32.

2. Beilby Porteus, *Death: A Poetical Essay* (Philadelphia, 1773), p. 20.

Chapter Four

1. See "Blake and Swedenborg" in Davies, pp. 31–53, for a good treatment of Blake's feelings about "this visionary."

2. The Swedenborgian resolutions are quoted from Davies, p. 34.

3. For an attempt to locate the issues at controversy, see John Howard, "An Audience for *The Marriage of Heaven and Hell*," *Blake Studies*, III (1970), 19–52.

4. Joseph Milner, quoted in Roland N. Stromberg, *Religious Liberalism in Eighteenth-Century England* (London, 1954), p. 168.

5. Stromberg, *Religious Liberalism in Eighteenth-Century England*, p. 173.

Chapter Five

1. The historical level of Blake's work is brilliantly explicated in David V. Erdman, *Blake: Prophet Against Empire*. Revised edition (Princeton, 1969).

2. See M. H. Abrams, "English Romanticism: The Spirit of the Age," in *Romanticism Reconsidered*, ed. Northrop Frye (New York, 1963), esp. pp. 30–37.

3. See Edmund Burke, "Reflections on the Revolution in France," in *Select Works*, ed. E. J. Payne (Oxford, n.d.), II, 89: "But the age of chivalry is gone. . . . Never, never more, shall we behold that generous loyalty to rank and sex, that proud submission, that dignified obedience, that subor-

dination of the heart, which kept alive, even in servitude itself, the spirit of an exalted freedom."

Chapter Seven

1. For a full discussion of the critical controversy surrounding the meaning of "The Tyger," and for a different reading of the poem, see Morton D. Paley, "Tyger of Wrath," PMLA, LXXXI (1966), 540–41.

2. Soame Jenyns, A Free Inquiry into the Nature and Origin of Evil (London, 1757), p. 179.

3. See, especially, "The Everlasting Gospel" (K 750–53).

4. The Marriage of Heaven and Hell (K 149).

5. See William Law, Selected Mystical Writings, ed. Stephen Hobhouse (London, 1938), p. 35: "Thinking and willing are eternal, they never began to be. Nothing can think or will now, in which there was not will and thought from all Eternity."; and p. 37: "And here you may behold the sure ground of the absolute impossibility of the annihilation of the soul."

6. Sir Paul Harvey, The Oxford Companion to English Literature, revised by Dorothy Eagle. Fourth edition (Oxford, 1967), p. 94.

Chapter Eight

1. Here, and throughout this book, I accept David Erdman's argument that Lambeth Palace "was in a sense the inner court of English Christianity. Indeed, Blake's tendency was to think of Lambeth as Christ's Bride, the Church. . . ." Erdman, "Lambeth and Bethlehem in Blake's Jerusalem," Modern Philology, XLVIII (1951), 184–92.

Chapter Eleven

1. Cf. Harold Bloom, Blake's Apocalypse (New York, 1963), p. 368, on "this mild song."

2. See S. Foster Damon, A Blake Dictionary, pp. 162–65, for a description, with an accompanying chart, of Golgonooza.

3. For Ephratah, see Damon, Blake Dictionary, p. 127. I equate Bethlehem ("City of the Woods in the Forest of Ephratah") and Lambeth, assuming that Blake considered Lambeth to mean "place of the Lamb," which was in fact an etymology put forward by a Dr. Ducarel in 1796. The subject is treated in Erdman's "Lambeth and Bethlehem in Blake's Jerusalem," 184–92, but Erdman does not equate Lambeth and Bethlehem.

4. The suggestion is made by William R. Hughes in his "simplified" edition of Jerusalem (London, 1964), p. 185: "The reference here is to Oxford as the nurse of poets and divines, and possibly also to the leaves of the Bible, the words of God which are printed there."

5. These are also the books of the Bible most admired by Swedenborg. See G. E. Bentley, Jr., "Blake and Swedenborg," Notes and Queries, CXCIX [n.s.] I (1954), 264–65, and Damon, Blake Dictionary, p. 45.

Conclusion

1. I do not, of course, limit the meaning of the term "post-modern" to the area of literary theory, but that aspect of Blake's "post-modernism" is treated very effectively in Hazard Adams, "Blake and the Postmodern," in *William Blake: Essays for S. Foster Damon*, pp. 3–17.

Selected Bibliography

This list has been pruned of outdated and redundant studies in the hope of providing a sound and minimal list for the student of Blake's work. Facsimiles of Blake's illuminated works, collections of his art work, and accounts of Blake the painter are excluded as inappropriate to the bibliography of a book so exclusively concerned as this one is with Blake the poet. The bibliographies cited below can be consulted for additional titles, as can the annual bibliographies of Romanticism published in *English Language Notes*.

PRIMARY SOURCES

ERDMAN, DAVID V. (ed.). *The Poetry and Prose of William Blake*. Commentary by Harold Bloom. Garden City: Doubleday, 1965. Now widely considered to be the standard scholarly edition of Blake. An outstanding job of editing.

KEYNES, GEOFFREY (ed.). *The Complete Writings of William Blake*. London: Oxford University Press, 1966. In its various editions (from 1925 on) this text was used by serious Blakists until the appearance of Erdman (above) in 1965. Now an alternate "standard" edition, it is preferred by many. Keynes's willingness to supply and regularize Blake's punctuation is a great help to all students of Blake, although this practice obviously results in a less faithful text than that supplied by Erdman.

———. *The Letters of William Blake*. London: Rupert Hart-Davis, 1968. The standard edition of the letters.

STEVENSON, W. H. (ed.). *The Poems of William Blake*. London: Longmans, 1971. Expertly annotated edition of the Erdman text of the poems; should prove extremely valuable for classroom use.

163

SECONDARY SOURCES

1. Bibliographies

BENTLEY, GERALD E., JR., and MARTIN K. NURMI. *A Blake Bibliography*. Minneapolis: University of Minnesota Press, 1964. Intelligently annotated and thoroughly useful compilation. Revised edition, ed. Bentley only, in press.

ERDMAN, DAVID V. "Blake." *English Poetry: Select Bibliographical Guides*. Ed. A. E. Dyson. London: Oxford University Press, 1971. Pp. 144–66. Excellent survey of books and periodical literature about Blake.

KEYNES, GEOFFREY. *A Bibliography of William Blake*. New York: The Grolier Club, 1921. Milestone in Blake scholarship; still of value for the specialist.

KEYNES, GEOFFREY, and EDWIN WOLF 2ND. *Blake's Illuminated Books: A Census*. New York: The Grolier Club, 1953. Catalogues and describes the works in illuminated printing.

TRAWICK, LEONARD M. "The Present State of Blake Studies." *Studies in Burke and His Time*, XII (1970), 1784–1803. An especially sound survey of recent work about Blake.

2. Biographies

BENTLEY, G. E., JR. *Blake Records*. Oxford: Clarendon Press, 1969. Expertly compiled, invaluable collection of the surviving documentary evidence about Blake as a man.

GILCHRIST, ALEXANDER. *Life of William Blake*. London: Macmillan, 1863. London: Dent, 1945. Most reliable of the few attempts that have been made to write a biography of Blake. Should now be supplemented with the materials available in *Blake Records* (above).

LISTER, RAYMOND. *William Blake: An Introduction to the Man and to His Work*. Foreword by G. E. Bentley, Jr. London: G. Bell and Sons, 1968. Enthusiastic biography by a man well qualified in the fine arts.

WILSON, MONA. *The Life of William Blake*. Edited by Geoffrey Keynes. London: Oxford University Press, 1971. Updating by Keynes of a sympathetic and generally accurate account of Blake the man. Suffers somewhat, however, from a forcing of the life into the patterns of "the Mystic Way." Previous editions in 1927 and 1948.

WITTREICH, JOSEPH ANTHONY, JR. (ed.). *Nineteenth-Century Accounts of William Blake*. Gainesville, Florida: Scholars' Facsimiles, 1970. Convenient collection of a few other attempts at writing the Blake biography.

3. Criticism

ADAMS, HAZARD. *William Blake: A Reading of the Shorter Poems*. Seattle: University of Washington Press, 1963. Important attempt to read Blake's lyrics from the perspective provided by reading his longer and more difficult works.

ALTIZER, THOMAS J. J. *The New Apocalypse: The Radical Christian Vision of William Blake*. East Lansing: Michigan State University Press, 1967. Study of Blake carried out by a major twentieth-century theologian. Attempt to explain Blake by means of Hegel seems unnecessarily oblique to the reader of Blake's poetry.

AULT, DONALD D. *Visionary Physics: Blake's Response to Newton*. Chicago: University of Chicago Press, 1974. Demonstrates way in which Blake interpreted Newtonian concepts and transformed them into poetic images.

BEER, JOHN. *Blake's Humanism*. Manchester: Manchester University Press, 1968. *Blake's Visionary Universe*. Manchester: Manchester University Press, 1969. Ambitious and generally successful attempt to describe Blake's thought and art.

BLACKSTONE, BERNARD. *English Blake*. Cambridge: Cambridge University Press, 1949. Sound study of many aspects of Blake's thought, especially in its relationship to Bacon, Newton, Locke, and Berkeley. However, like many other excellent Blakists, Blackstone tends to ignore the extent to which Blake's Christianity is both literal and traditional.

BLOOM, HAROLD. *Blake's Apocalypse*. Garden City: Doubleday, 1963. Brilliant critic's poem-by-poem presentation of Blake with special emphasis on Blake's achievement as an epic poet.

BRONOWSKI, JACOB. *William Blake and the Age of Revolution*. New York: Harper and Row, 1965. Attractive account of Blake's life and times but marred by an over-insistence on Blake as anti-industrialist. The book is a "new edition" of Bronowski's *William Blake: A Man Without a Mask* (London: Secker & Warburg, 1944), but actually adds only a new introduction.

CURRAN, STUART, and JOSEPH ANTHONY WITTREICH, JR. (eds.). *Blake's Sublime Allegory: Essays on "The Four Zoas," "Milton," and "Jerusalem."* Madison: University of Wisconsin Press, 1973. Essays evaluate both the visual and the poetic aspects of Blake's achievement.

DAMON, S. FOSTER. *William Blake: His Philosophy and Symbols*. Boston: Houghton Mifflin, 1924. Pioneer work in Blake criticism. The information on Blake's sources and on the symbolic meaning of his mythic figures provides the foundation for all subsequent readings of Blake — even though Damon's judgments are very often highly intuitive.

DAVIES, J. G. *The Theology of William Blake.* Oxford: Clarendon Press, 1948. Careful, usually accurate report on Blake's religious opinions; but has not had sufficient attention from Blake scholars.

DORFMAN, DEBORAH. *Blake in the Nineteenth Century: His Reputation as a Poet from Gilchrist to Yeats.* New Haven: Yale University Press, 1969. There were a few significant exceptions to the neglect Blake's work suffered until very recent times; and Dorfman usefully documents them in this study.

ERDMAN, DAVID V. *Blake: Prophet Against Empire.* Revised Edition. Princeton: Princeton University Press, 1969. A triumph of research, this book convincingly demonstrates Blake's extensive use of the events and moods of his own age.

ERDMAN, DAVID V., and JOHN E. GRANT (eds.). *Blake's Visionary Forms Dramatic.* Princeton: Princeton University Press, 1969. Collection of essays that focus on the pictorial side of Blake's creativity. Taken together, these essays form the best treatment of this aspect of Blake's achievement.

FISHER, PETER F. *The Valley of Vision.* Ed. Northrop Frye. Toronto: University of Toronto Press, 1961. Major study of Blake's thought from a history of ideas perspective.

FROSCH, THOMAS R. *The Awakening of Albion: The Renovation of the Body in the Poetry of William Blake.* Ithaca: Cornell University Press, 1974. Exploration of "Albion's resumption of consciousness and of Blake's participation in the Romantic spirit of a complete human renewal, a spirit fundamentally secular. . . ."

FRYE, NORTHROP. *Fearful Symmetry: A Study of William Blake.* Princeton: Princeton University Press, 1947. First book to offer a fully coherent picture of Blake's over-all philosophy and esthetic. The best book on Blake.

————. "The Keys to the Gates." *Some British Romantics.* Ed. James V. Logan, John E. Jordan, and Northrop Frye. Columbus: Ohio State University Press, 1966. Outstanding but quite brief account of Blake's "system."

GARDNER, STANLEY. *Blake.* London: Evans Brothers, 1968. Remarkable for the achievement of a good sense of Blake's presence as a Londoner. Omits consideration of Blake's epics; offers some good independent readings of the shorter poems.

GLECKNER, ROBERT. *The Piper and the Bard.* Detroit: Wayne State University Press, 1959. Good study of the lyrics and of the concepts of Innocence and Experience.

HAGSTRUM, JEAN H. *William Blake: Poet and Painter.* Chicago: University of Chicago Press, 1964. Pioneer attempt to interpret the "composite art" of Blake's illuminated works.

HARPER, GEORGE MILLS. *The Neoplatonism of William Blake.* Chapel Hill: University of North Carolina Press, 1961. Interesting argument for the possible influence on Blake of Thomas Taylor, a contemporary Neo-Platonic thinker. Kathleen Raine is one major Blakist sympathetic to Harper's position; otherwise, few find it useful to study Blake in these terms.

HIRSCH, E. D., JR. *Innocence and Experience: An Introduction to Blake.* New Haven: Yale University Press, 1964. Attempt to demonstrate the development of Blake's thought and to deny that Blake's work has the monolithic coherence seen by Frye and most other critics. This argument has generally been ignored.

KROEBER, KARL. "Graphic-Poetic Structuring in Blake's *Book of Urizen.*" *Blake Studies,* III (Fall, 1970), 7–18. Best brief account of the esthetic issues raised in Blake's unique artistic production, the illuminated "narrative." Good supplement to the material in the Erdman and Grant collection and in the Hagstrum book.

LOWERY, MARGARET R. *Windows of the Morning: A Critical Study of William Blake's "Poetical Sketches."* New Haven: Yale University Press, 1940. Useful study of Blake's emergence from his eighteenth-century poetic milieu.

MELLOR, ANNE KOSTELANETZ. *Blake's Human Form Divine.* Berkeley: University of California, 1974. Study of Blake's "visual verbal art" finds "conflict between his philosophical theory and artistic practice, between his philosophical rejection of the human body and his aesthetic glorification of the human figure."

NURMI, MARTIN K. *William Blake.* London: Hutchinson, 1975. Impressive brief study.

PALEY, MORTON D. *Energy and the Imagination.* Oxford: Clarendon Press, 1970. Intelligent, well-informed study of what are perhaps the two crucial concepts in Blake's thought.

PALEY, MORTON D., and MICHAEL PHILLIPS (eds.). *William Blake: Essays in Honour of Sir Geoffrey Keynes.* Oxford: Clarendon Press, 1973. "The essays in this volume range in subject-matter from the earliest of Blake's writings and art to the works and friendships of his last years and the vicissitudes of his posthumous reputation."

RAINE, KATHLEEN. *Blake and Tradition.* Princeton: Princeton University Press for the Bollingen Foundation, 1968. Two volumes. The product of a lifelong study of Blake and of the "heterodox tradition" in religion and philosophy, these handsome volumes set forth significant analogues and sources for Blake's art and ideas. As with Damon, another specialist in the heterodox, a few of the conclusions seem overly intuitive.

ROSENFELD, ALVIN H. (ed.). *William Blake: Essays for S. Foster Damon.* Providence: Brown University Press, 1969. Handsome tribute to a widely influential Blakist and a fascinating sampling of the interests of some outstanding scholars who continue Damon's work.

SCHORER, MARK. *William Blake: The Politics of Vision.* New York: Holt,

1946. Although the book is especially good on the political contexts of
Blake's thought, it also serves the general reader as a sound introduction to most of Blake's related concerns.

SINGER, JUNE K. *The Unholy Bible: A Psychological Interpretation of
William Blake*. New York: G. P. Putnam's Sons for the C. G. Jung
Foundation, 1970. A Jungian study of Blake is a good idea, but this
book accepts too many of the biographical legends about Blake to be
at all convincing to the Blake scholar.

WAGENKNECHT, DAVID. *Blake's Night: William Blake and the Idea of
Pastoral*. Cambridge: Harvard University Press, 1973. Studies Blake's
poetry "in terms of a single, unifying thematic concern or idea: the
idea of pastoral."

WITTREICH, JOSEPH ANTHONY, JR. *Angel of Apocalypse: Blake's Idea of
Milton*. Madison: University of Wisconsin Press, 1975. "As a critic of
Milton, Blake is peerless: his understanding far outruns the under-
standing of Milton that dominated the nineteenth century. . . ."

4. Reference

DAMON, S. FOSTER. *A Blake Dictionary*. Providence: Brown University
Press, 1965. A study of Blake's philosophy and symbols presented in
"dictionary" format by the father of American Blake studies. Also
available in paperback (New York: E. P. Dutton, 1971).

ERDMAN, DAVID V. *A Concordance to the Writings of William Blake*. Ithaca:
Cornell University Press, 1967. Two volumes.

Index

(The works of William Blake are listed under his name)

Bacon, Francis, 30, 50, 75, 143, 144, 150, 154
Basire, James, 17, 22
Bentley, G. E., Jr., 26
Berkeley, Bishop, 58, 59, 96
Blake, Catherine Boucher, 19, 23, 27, 28
Blake, James, 26
Blake, Robert, 22
Blake, William, life and times, 15 - 28

WORKS:
All Religions Are One, 22, 23, 32
America, 61, *68 - 69*
"Auguries of Innocence," 113
Book of Ahania, The, 25, 47
Book of Los, The, 25, 47
Book of Thel, The, *85 - 86*, 96, 152
Book of Urizen, The, 25, 29, *34 - 45*, 46, 47, 86, 88, 90, 91, 98, 100, 121, 139, 152
"Crystal Cabinet, The," 114, *117 - 18*
Descriptive Catalogue, The, 26
Europe, 25, 47
Four Zoas, The, 25, 29, 40, 47, 78, *88 - 112*, 113, 114, 152
French Revolution, The, 24, 29, *61 - 68*, 69, *103*, 104, 153
"Golden Net, The," 114
Illustrations to the Book of Job, 27
Island in the Moon, An, 21 - 22
Jerusalem, 24, 25, 26, 27, 47, 88, 119, *133 - 51*, 152
Marriage of Heaven and Hell, The, *53 - 60*, 78, 81, 119, 153

"Mental Traveller, The," 61, *114 - 16*, 117
Milton, 24, 25, 26, 27, 79 - 80, 88, *119 - 32*, 137, 152
Poetical Sketches, 21, 29, *48 - 52*
"Fair Elenor," 20
"Fresh from the Dewy Hill," 49
"Gwin, King of Norway," 20, *51 - 52*
"How sweet I roam'd," 50
"King Edward the Third," 20, 52
"Mad Song," 50
"To Autumn," 49
"To Spring," 49
"To Summer," 49
"To the Evening Star," 48
"To the Muses," 50
"To Winter," 49
Songs of Experience, The, 74, 77 - 86, 87, 113, 153
"Chimney Sweeper, The," 82
"Earth's Answer," 78
"Fly, The," 84
"Garden of Love, The," 82
"Holy Thursday," 77
"Infant Sorrow," 81
"Lilly, The," 83
"Little Boy Lost, The," 83
"Little Girl Found, The," 79, 80
"Little Girl Lost, The," 80
"London," 80 - 81
"Schoolboy, The," 82
"To Tirzah," 84, 86, 87
"Tyger, The," 78 - 79, 95, 101, 153

169

Songs of Innocence and of Experience,
    25, *74 - 85*
Songs of Innocence, 22, 24, 48 - 49,
    74 - 77, 80, 82, 113, 153
    "Chimney Sweeper, The," *75 - 76*,
        82
    "Cradle Song, A," 75
    "Dream, A," 75
    "Holy Thursday," 22, *76 - 77*
    "Lamb, The," 75
    "Little Black Boy, The," 76
    "Little Boy Found, The," 75
    "Little Boy Lost, The," 22, 75
    "Nurse's Song," 22, 75
    "On Another's Sorrow," 75
    "Shepherd, The," 75
Song of Los, The, 47
There Is No Natural Religion, 17, 22,
    23, *30 - 32*
Tiriel, 86 - 87
Vala. See *Four Zoas, The*.
Vision of The Last Judgment, The,
    29, 31
Visions of the Daughters of Albion,
    25, 29, *70 - 73*, 96, 102, 123, 153
Bloom, Harold, 33
Boehme, Jacob, 15, 16, 54
Bolingbroke, Henry St. John, Viscount,
    131
Boucher, Catherine. *See* Blake, Catherine
    Boucher.
Burke, Edmund, 24, 62, 64
Butts, Thomas, 27, 29
Byron, George Gordon, Lord, 20, 97,
    147

Calvin, John, 127
Chaucer, Geoffrey, 150
Chew, Samuel C., 20
Christian Perfection (Law), 16
Clowes, John, 23
Coleridge, Samuel Taylor, 15, 20, 88,
    154
Cowper, William, 50

Damon, S. Foster, 34
Dante, 54, 88, 154
Death: A Poetical Essay (Porteus), 51

Divine Comedy (Dante), 88
Dürer, Albert, 18

Fall of Hyperion (Keats), 88
Fenelon, François, 144
Flaxman, John, 21
Frye, Northrop, 34, 154

Gardner, Stanley, 17, 48
Gibbon, Edward, 131, 141
Gladstone, William, 16, 23
Godwin, William, 24, 62
Guyon, Madame, 144

Hartley, T., 23
Hayley, William, 25, 134
Hervey, James, 144
Hume, David, 90, 131, 147, 154
Hunt, Robert, 26, 134
Hyperion (Keats), 88

Jenyns, Soame, 82
Johnson, Joseph, 24, 61, 62
Johnson, Samuel, 96

Keats, John, 88, 117
Keynes, Geoffrey, 30, 88, 103

Law, William, 16
Lawrence, D. H., 59, 117
Locke, John, 30, 50, 121, 136, 143, 144,
    150, 154
Luther, Martin, 127, 145

Mathew, A. S., 21, 52
Mathew, Harriet, 21
Milner, Joseph, 55
Milton, John, 34, 46, 55, 56, 60, 65,
    119 - 32, 150, 154. *See also:* Blake,
    William, WORKS: *Milton*.

Newton, Isaac, 50, 121, 128, 130, 136,
    143, 144, 150, 154
Night Thoughts (Young), 25
Nurmi, Martin K., 20

Paine, Thomas, 24, 62, 118, 153
Paracelsus, 15, 54

Paradise Lost (Milton), 65, 88, 121
Paradise Regained (Milton), 119
Parker, James, 22
Plato, 59
Political Justice (Godwin), 24, 62
Porteus, Beilby, 51
Prelude, The (Wordsworth), 88
Price, Richard, 24, 62
Priestley, Joseph, 62

Reynolds, Joshua, 18, 55
Rights of Man (Paine), 24, 62
Rime of the Ancient Mariner, The (Coleridge), 88
Robinson, H. Crabb, 27
Rose, Samuel, 26
Rousseau, 67, 113, 131, 141

Scolfield, John, 25, 134
Serious Call, A (Law), 16
Shakespeare, William, 54, 150
Sharp, William, 23

Shelley, Percy, 15, 20
Shepherd, T. B., 16
Siris (Bérkeley), 58
Socrates, 56
Southcott, Joanna, 23
Swedenborg, Emanuel, 23, 53, 54, 56, 60

Taylor, Thomas, 15
Theresa of Avila, 144
Thomson, James, 20
Truchsess, Joseph, Count, 26

Voltaire, 67, 113, 118, 131, 141, 144, 153

Wesley, John, 16, 126, 127
Whitefield, George, 16, 126, 127, 141, 144
Wood, Polly, 19
Wordsworth, William, 15, 88, 154

Young, Edward, 25